PENGUIN PASSNOTES

A Man for all Seasons

Susan Quilliam was born in Liverpool and read Psychology and English at Liverpool University. After a period of teaching she moved to London where she now works as a freelance writer, as well as a counsellor. She has written a number of study guides in the Penguin Passnotes series, including *Silas Marner*, *Roots* and *Pride and Prejudice*, and her book *Positive Smear* will be published by Penguin in 1989.

PENGUIN PASSNOTES

ROBERT BOLT

A Man for All Seasons

SUSAN QUILLIAM
ADVISORY EDITOR: STEPHEN COOTE, M.A., PH.D.

PENGUIN BOOKS

PENGUIN BOOKS

Published by the Penguin Group
27 Wrights Lane, London W8 5TZ, England
Viking Penguin Inc., 40 West 23rd Street, New York, New York 10010, USA
Penguin Books Australia Ltd, Ringwood, Victoria, Australia
Penguin Books Canada Ltd, 2801 John Street, Markham, Ontario, Canada L3R 1B4
Penguin Books (NZ) Ltd, 182–190 Wairau Road, Auckland 10, New Zealand

Penguin Books Ltd, Registered Offices: Harmondsworth, Middlesex, England

First published 1985
10 9 8 7 6 5 4 3

Made and printed in Great Britain by
Richard Clay Ltd, Bungay, Suffolk
Filmset in Monophoto Ehrhardt

Contents

To the Student

This book is designed to help you with your GCSE English Literature examination. It contains a synopsis of the plot, a glossary of the more unfamiliar words and phrases, and a commentary on some of the issues raised by the text. An account of the writer's life is also included for background.

Page references in parentheses are to the edition published by Heinemann Educational Books Ltd, with a Preface by Robert Bolt.

When you use this book, remember that it is no more than an aid to your study. It will help you find passages quickly and perhaps give you some ideas for essays. But remember: *This book is not a substitute for reading the text and it is your knowledge and your response that matter*. These are the things the examiners are looking for, and they are also the things that will give you the most pleasure. Show your knowledge and appreciation to the examiner, and show them clearly.

Introduction: Robert Bolt and A Man for All Seasons

Why did Robert Bolt, writing in the latter half of the twentieth century, take as his subject a martyr of the sixteenth century? Was the appeal historical – the pull of an age and a way of thinking other than his own? The answer must be no. The issues about which Bolt wrote his play on the life and death of Sir Thomas More were certainly those of the Tudor age, but the underlying pattern of thought is very much Bolt's own.

Robert Bolt was born in Manchester in 1924, and attended Manchester Grammar School. He did not fulfil his potential at school, and on leaving, he went to work as a junior in an insurance office. Later, however, he went to Manchester University to read History, followed this with a year at Exeter University, and then became a teacher, rising to the position of Head of the English Department at Millfield School.

Bolt's interest in ethical issues – what is good, what is bad, how we should act in response to what we believe – was constantly developing. In particular, he gave his support to the Campaign for Nuclear Disarmament, feeling very concerned about the growing use of nuclear weapons.

While teaching, Robert Bolt also wrote a number of radio plays which were broadcast, and in 1958, when one of his works, *The Flowering Cherry*, was successful in London, he decided to give up teaching and concentrate on his writing. By 1960, his gamble had paid off: he had two plays in the West End at the same time, and offers of film and theatre work were pouring in.

A Man for All Seasons is Robert Bolt's major triumph to date. It was first performed in London in July 1960, with Paul Scofield in the title role, as he was also in the later film version. It has been produced many times all over the world, and was voted Best Foreign Play of 1962 in New York.

The play's main topic – a man who sticks to his principles despite overwhelming personal and political pressure – comes directly from Bolt's own philosophy. We know from his writings that Bolt chose More not only as dramatically appealing, and as an intelligent, educated Tudor man, but also because he deeply admired More's thoughts and actions. On one occasion, Bolt himself was arrested during a disarmament demonstration and put in jail; but he was soon released and bound over to keep the peace. Afterwards, he admitted wishing that he had stayed in jail, rather than submitting to pressure not to continue the campaign. To him, this showed a lack of commitment to his beliefs.

Thomas More's beliefs led him far further than jail, and he kept to his principles regardless. We can see how Bolt's admiration and fascination for such a man arose, and why he wished to write a play which would show to the world a comprehensive view of More and explain his actions. The issues are specific to the Tudor age; the commitment is not. So Bolt chose a historical figure in order to express his own twentieth-century view of commitment and responsibility, and present it to a modern audience.

Synopsis

Act One

The play is introduced (p. 1) by the Common Man, who first takes the part of Steward to Sir Thomas More (p. 1).

The scene is Sir Thomas More's house. Thomas enters with Richard Rich, who is discussing possible ways to 'buy a man' (p. 2). Rich's views lead More to warn the younger man that his stay in London is leading him into bad company – Cromwell, for instance. Rich, however, is only interested in progressing politically (p. 3), even when More points out to him the temptations of power, by giving Rich a goblet which has been offered to More himself as a bribe (p. 4).

Now More's wife Alice, his daughter Margaret and his friend Norfolk enter, arguing about falconry (p. 5). When all turn their attention to Rich and learn he is acquainted with Cromwell, Norfolk breaks the worrying news that this unscrupulous man has been appointed Secretary to Cardinal Wolsey, Lord Chancellor (p. 6).

At this point, a summons comes from Wolsey. More says good-night to his family, who end the evening with a prayer (p. 7). Norfolk and More leave, and Rich lags behind to take with him the goblet (p. 9). The Steward completes the scene, changing it to Wolsey's palace.

Wolsey has just prepared a letter to send to the Pope, requesting a divorce for the King. He shows it to More (p. 10), who tactfully refuses to comment; they discuss Henry's dilemma, More's position (pp. 11–12) and the question of who will succeed Wolsey as Chancellor (p. 13).

Leaving Wolsey (p. 13), More goes to find a boat to take him home. He is first approached by Cromwell (p. 14), then by Chapuys, the Spanish ambassador (p. 15). Both wish to know what his views on the marriage are. He tells neither of them anything, and leaves for home.

Arriving there (p. 16), More finds his daughter Margaret with William Roper, who has come to ask for her hand in marriage. More refuses this (p. 17) because Roper's religious views are opposed to those of the Catholic Church. When Roper has left, both Margaret and Alice ask More about his conversation with Wolsey (pp. 18–19), but he parries their questions.

The Common Man now shows us the passage of time and events by announcing the death of Wolsey and the appointment of More as Chancellor (p. 20).

The scene changes to Hampton Court, where Cromwell and Rich are joined by Chapuys. Cromwell has risen in power (p. 21) to be close to the King, who is shortly to preside over the launch of a new warship (p. 22). Then the Common Man enters as the Steward, and both Cromwell and Chapuys question him about More's attitude to the King's divorce plans (pp. 23–4).

The scene changes to More's house. More's family is looking for him, because the King is to visit while launching the new ship (p. 25).

More has been to church and arrives just in time (p. 26). King Henry appears (p. 27). He greets More's family (p. 28), and arranges to stay for supper (p. 29). Then he and Thomas draw aside to talk.

Henry soon speaks of Wolsey and his failure to obtain the divorce (p. 30). Then he asks Thomas again for his view, and is angry when More speaks against the plan (p. 31). The King needs More's support (p. 32) and says he will have no opposition (p. 33).

Henry leaves, sooner than expected (p. 34), to the family's unease (p. 35). Will Roper has arrived and wishes to explain to Thomas how his religious views have changed; More tells him not to criticize the King's actions (p. 36), for this would be treason. In the midst of this, Rich enters. He warns Thomas of Cromwell's and Chapuys's interest in him and asks More to employ him. More refuses (pp. 37–8).

When Rich leaves, Roper and Thomas discuss the law. More, worried about Roper's changing views, explains his belief in the law, religion and principles as stable forces (pp. 38–40). Finally the More family go off to eat dinner (p. 41).

The Common Man appears, to mark the change of scene. He takes the part of a publican at an inn where Cromwell is meeting Rich (p. 42). Cromwell has just been appointed Secretary to the Council; he begins by hinting to Rich the possibilities of his having an influential position too (pp. 43–4), if only he will divulge a little information. He asks Rich about the goblet More gave him (p. 45); Rich tells him, and they discuss the possibility of frightening More into agreeing with the divorce (pp. 45–6).

Act Two

The Common Man explains that two years have passed; it is now 1532. In the meantime, Henry has set in motion the Act of Parliament founding the Church of England (p. 47).

More and Roper are discussing the turn of events (p. 47). Will, once fiercely against the Catholic Church, now equally stubbornly defends it. More is waiting to hear whether the Catholic bishops have accepted the Act (p. 48).

Chapuys enters (p. 49), to discuss the Act with More, who is wary, and will not state his views (p. 50). Chapuys is offering More support from the rebellious Northern Catholics, when Norfolk arrives (p. 51). He tells More that the Convocation of the bishops has submitted to the Act. More, feeling he can no longer serve as Chancellor, immediately removes his chain of office, much to the distress of Alice and Norfolk, who argue with him (pp. 52–3). In the end, defeated, Norfolk tells More that the King accepts his resignation; More passes on to Norfolk the information Chapuys gave him about rebellion in the North (p. 54).

When Norfolk leaves, More turns to his family. Roper (now married to Meg) admires him (p. 55), but Alice is insulted that he will not explain his actions, until More reminds her of the danger involved (p. 56). They prepare to tell the servants the news of More's resignation, hoping some will stay, on lower wages, but unresentful if they do not (p. 57).

In the next scene, Norfolk and Cromwell are discussing More's actions; Cromwell is hoping to discredit him by proving him guilty of accepting bribes (p. 58). The woman who gave More the goblet appears, and she and Richard Rich give evidence (p. 59); but Norfolk successfully quashes the charge (p. 60). Left alone, Cromwell and Rich, whose fortunes are rising, determine to beat More (p. 61).

Chapuys visits the impoverished More household (p. 62). He wishes to give Thomas a letter from the Spanish King (p. 63), but More, knowing that any suspicion of siding with Spain would destroy him, refuses. When Chapuys leaves (p. 64), Alice berates Thomas for the poverty they are suffering (p. 65).

Roper enters, with the news that More is summoned to appear before Cromwell (p. 65). With Rich as scribe, Cromwell questions More, first about his dealings with the 'Holy Maid of Kent', a traitor (p. 67), then about his contribution to the King's book *A Defence of the Seven Sacraments* (pp. 68–9). Finally, Cromwell asks More directly about his views concerning the King's marriage (p. 69). More refuses to answer, and Cromwell lets him go, but comments to Rich that More must bless the marriage or be destroyed (p. 70).

More cannot find a boatman to row him home, as his reputation is now so ruined. Norfolk meets him by the river (p. 70) and pleads with him to change his mind and give his approval to the King's actions (p. 71). More gently refuses, then, realizing that remaining friends would be dangerous for Norfolk, provokes a quarrel (pp. 72–3). Norfolk leaves.

Now Margaret and Roper enter, with the news that the King has proposed an Act of Parliament, with an oath, supporting the marriage (pp. 73–4). More is frightened, but still hopeful that he can avoid the charge of treason.

The scene changes to the Tower; More has obviously been imprisoned for not taking the oath. The Common Man, acting as Jailer (p. 75), tells us at this point how Cromwell, Norfolk, King Henry and Richard Rich ended their days.

Then the Jailer goes to wake the sleeping More, taking him to be questioned by Cromwell, Cranmer and Norfolk (p. 76). They demand that More swear to the Act, and he refuses, but he will not tell them why (p. 77). Thus they can only guess that his objections are treasonable and cannot legally execute him (p. 78). Norfolk appeals to him to swear, and Thomas gently refuses. Cromwell threatens, but More stands firm (p. 79).

When More has returned to his cell, Cromwell attempts to bribe the Jailer into revealing any information he overhears from More (p. 80), and then again tells Rich that, whatever the price, More must submit, for the King's peace of mind (p. 81).

Back in the cell, Thomas is visited by his family. They are appalled at the conditions he is in; he is ecstatic to see them (p. 82). Then he learns that they have been allowed to visit only in order to persuade him to take the oath (p. 83). Meg and More argue through the logic of it. In the end, defeated, she can only try to pressure him by telling him what his family is suffering (p. 84).

Then More turns to Alice; at first, she is cold, not understanding what he is doing (p. 85), but in the end, their love breaks through, and she supports him (p. 86). As he turns back to the others, the Jailer enters and, despite their protests, makes the family leave (pp. 87–8).

The scene is set for the trial. The Common Man takes the part of the Foreman of the Jury. Cromwell announces the trial, and Norfolk and Cranmer enter to preside. Cromwell reads the charge, denying King Henry his title of head of the Church of England, which is high treason. More repeats his argument that silence is not denial (p. 90). Cromwell now argues to the jury that there are many different kinds of silence (p. 91), while More responds with the legal maxim that 'Silence Gives Consent' (p. 92).

Now Sir Richard Rich gives evidence (p. 93). He states under oath that, in conversation with him, More denied that the Act of Supremacy was legal, and therefore denied that the King was head of the Church – an act of treason (p. 94).

More, realizing now what is happening, fights back – swearing that Rich lies, arguing that this evidence is logically unsound, calling for other witnesses. Finally, he realizes that he cannot win (p. 95). He rejects a final offer of leniency from the King if he will sign, and then makes his last speech before sentence (p. 96). In it, he condemns the Act of Supremacy, though he is sure that the real reason for his death

is because he will not approve the marriage. Norfolk reads the sentence
– death (p. 97).

The scene changes to a place of execution, with the Common Man
acting as Headsman. One by one, the characters say goodbye to
Thomas – Norfolk who betrayed him, Margaret who supported him,
the woman who tried to bribe him, Cranmer the churchman who
submitted where Thomas would not (pp. 98–9).

More is executed, and the executioner displays his head (p. 99). The
final scene of the play has two variations: in one Cromwell and Chapuys
exit together, the survivors; in the other (p. 100), the Common Man
makes a rueful comment on the play, before saying good-night to the
audience.

An Account of the Plot

Bolt prefaces his play with two quotations concerning Thomas More, stressing his intelligence, education, goodness and flexibility. The first quotation includes the title phrase 'a man for all seasons', which crystallizes Bolt's view of his leading character (see pp. 69–72).

'PEOPLE IN THE PLAY'

The list of characters is not simple. It also gives features of each character's external appearance and internal personality which the playwright considers important. Notice that, unlike many playwrights, Bolt is here describing real people, adding to what we already know about them historically by interpretations of his own. In the case of the Common Man, the person described is a 'type' – a generalization. Further comments on the characters are given later in this book (pp. 52–72).

'THE SET' AND 'THE COSTUMES'

Bolt's approach to the play states clearly and in some detail how he visualizes the scenery and design. Try to keep this clearly in mind while studying the text, and do not confuse Bolt's idea of the play with other versions you may have seen on stage or screen.

The set is simple, with a double gallery and stairs. It does not change throughout the play, and presents a neutral backdrop to which other elements are added to create specific locations – the river, the inn, the jail and so on.

The costumes, it is stated, do not need to be historically accurate – this is not Bolt's concern. He specifies which colours could reflect each character – scarlet for the Cardinal, for example, and the richest colour, gold, for the King.

ACT ONE

Act One opens with the Common Man. He speaks directly to the audience, saying how odd it is that, in a play full of important and elaborately dressed nobles, he should begin. As it is, he is simply wearing black – just enough to cover his nakedness, that part of him which is unmistakably himself. He puts on a hat and coat from the property basket, assuming the character of Sir Thomas More's Steward. The scene becomes Sir Thomas's house.

Surreptitiously, the Steward tastes the wine. As he does so, he comments that he is of the sixteenth century, the 'Century of the Common Man'; but then all centuries are influenced not only by important people but also by ordinary folk.

Notice that Bolt chooses to open the play with the Common Man because he, as much as any of the major characters, is responsible for what happens; he speaks to us, and also for us. We too create history.

Next, Sir Thomas More enters. The Steward Matthew points him out to us, and More asks him for the wine. Knowing that Matthew has almost certainly tasted it, More asks him if the wine is good, but the Steward innocently denies all knowledge, and More lets this pass.

He turns back again to his discussion with Richard Rich. Rich is certain that everyone can be bought, but More argues that some men will not sell their beliefs. Rich then suggests buying a man with suffering; More is momentarily interested in the thought that some may be tempted by martyrdom, until he realizes that Rich means that if a man is made to suffer and then offered a way out, he will take it, whatever the price.

At this point, More challenges Rich that he has been reading the work of Machiavelli, an Italian philosopher whose ideas concerning ruthless power were new to England. Rich is embarrassed, for the idea of reading Machiavelli has come through Cromwell, whose reputation in More's household is poor. However, Cromwell has promised him advancement, which is more than he has yet achieved since being in London. More is worried for Rich: he realizes that the young man wants only money and power, and will trade his principles for them. Instead, he should go back to Cambridge to study, where he will be safe, away from the temptations of London's rich society. An alternative would be to take a post as a teacher at the new St Paul's School. But Rich despises teaching; he wants to make his name at Court.

More tries to prove his point to Rich by giving him a silver goblet, which Rich readily accepts. Then More reveals that the goblet was a bribe from a woman whose lawsuit is due to appear before More. To keep the cup would be to lay himself open to charges of corruption, so More gives it to Rich. He warns the young man that such attempted bribes are common when one is in office, and again advises him seriously to be a teacher – he has the talent for it. Rich, more concerned with fame than fulfilment, cannot accept this advice.

This scene between Rich and More immediately establishes several of the main themes of the play. They are discussing whether a man can be bought: Rich, we later see, can, while More keeps to his principles through suffering even to death. The whole area of how to live one's life in terms of achievement and gain is examined too, and we see through Rich how his wish to be accepted in society has begun to contaminate him. On the other hand, More is not worried by what other people think.

The personality of the main character is apparent from the start. More is intelligent, human, warm and sympathetic to the weaknesses of both Rich and Matthew, yet firm to his principles. He sees at once what sort of person Rich is, and tries to persuade him into the right occupation. He himself is doing his inspired best in a public office because his King commanded it. Conversely, Rich is as yet an innocent man, but is on the verge of being corrupted. He is weak and easily influenced. In many ways he is the total opposite to More.

The next section begins with the entry of Alice, Norfolk and Margaret, all announced to the audience by the Steward. Alice and Norfolk are arguing about whether a falcon, flying in cloud, could see clearly enough to stoop (drop) on its prey. Alice, disbelieving Norfolk's claim about his falcon's being able to do this, appeals to More, who tactfully refuses to get involved. Rich tries to intervene with a comment on philosophy aimed at impressing Norfolk. In the end, Norfolk challenges Alice to ride with him to see the falcon perform, to which she agrees stubbornly, though More is shocked at the idea, and tells her he thinks she will be proved wrong.

This small section introduces the stubborn and brave Alice, sensitive Margaret and aristocratic Norfolk. It establishes our picture of More with his family – mild, genuinely concerned for both Alice and Margaret, at ease in both light and philosophical conversation.

Rich's comment draws their attention to him. More mentions that the young man has been reading Machiavelli; Norfolk disapproves, though Margaret considers the book 'practical' (p. 7). This proof of her intelligence leads Norfolk to compliment her, but wonder where she will ever find a husband.

Rich's comments on Machiavelli lead him to mention Cromwell, at which Norfolk says that Cromwell has just been appointed Secretary to the Cardinal. More and his family are shocked that such a ruthless man should be appointed to such an influential post. Thomas asks Rich whether he knew the news, and while Rich denies it, he nevertheless admits to liking Cromwell. More comments that if Rich gets on well with the man, he will rise fast now that Cromwell has power.

The Steward appears, with a letter for More summoning him to an immediate meeting with Cardinal Wolsey. Alice comments sharply that it is no doubt about the 'Queen's business' (p. 8) – the divorce. Thomas cuts across any possible treacherous comments, then leads the family in a prayer.

The section about More's family once again is set against a reminder that, in the background, evil is at work. Cromwell has risen in power, and is beginning to be dangerous. We also see too Rich's changeability in order to impress Norfolk and his almost inexorable movement towards the temptations Cromwell offers.

The party splits up. More points out to Norfolk that Rich needs employment, but honestly says: 'I don't recommend him' (p. 8). Then, with jokes about hawking, they all say good-night.

Rich returns to collect his goblet, nervously justifying himself to the Steward. The Steward flatters Rich, who gives him money – but once Rich has gone, Matthew comments disparagingly about him. He concludes the scene, while he packs the props away, by saying that as in the case of Rich and the goblet, Thomas More will give anything to anybody. This is dangerous, for there may be something More doesn't want to give away and 'he'll be out of practice' (p. 9).

The focus of the play turns again from family to outside matters. More's attempt to get Rich a clerical post and Rich's own fall into temptation by taking the goblet show the corruption existing outside the More family which will ultimately affect them. More honestly does his best for Rich, but warns him of the dangers – and warns Norfolk of the dangers of employing him. Rich is seen more clearly in his relationship with the Steward which develops during the course of the play.

The scene changes to Wolsey's palace. The Cardinal is impatient because More is late. He wishes More to read a dispatch before he sends it to the Vatican. More makes a non-committal comment, but then he admits to his disapproval of the document enough to suggest that the King's Council be allowed to read it. Wolsey impatiently asks Thomas if he will 'help' (support the divorce) without letting his morals intrude.

Suddenly, a trumpet sounds. The two men watch from the window as the King passes, on his way back from seeing Anne Boleyn. Then Wolsey speaks to Thomas directly: the King needs a son and if there is no son, the Tudor dynasty ends. Is that what Thomas wants? More is appalled at this suggestion that he is a traitor. But he cannot agree to a proposal of divorce. Catherine is Henry's wife, whether she is fertile or not. The Pope has already ruled that Henry and Catherine may marry; he alone can unmake that ruling, so why not ask him? Wolsey suggests pressurizing the Pope by suggestions of revolt; More disagrees. Wolsey reminds him of the horrendous wars that ensued last time there was uncertainty about succession. How can More, by opposing an attempt to give Henry an heir, open that possibility? More replies that he cannot forsake his conscience.

Wolsey closes the conversation by wondering who will succeed him as Chancellor. More votes for Bishop Fisher, Wolsey wonders about Cromwell. Their final words are an ironic comment on More's real holiness and Wolsey's practical worldliness.

This short scene takes us fully into the political situation around which the play revolves. Wolsey explains the situation, More explains his opposition.

Wolsey, a Cardinal of the Church, is in fact less moral than More, a layman who believes in following his conscience. Wolsey is concerned for the public good, aware of (and despising) the King's wants, and interested in his own survival. Thomas realizes that the public good is made up of individual men's morality. He overrules the King's (and his own) wants, though he refuses to criticize the King. He places his own survival and advancement below his own beliefs, standing fast against persuasion, threats and Wolsey's corrupt power.

More's journey home is made by river; the lighting and scenery reflect this. He calls a Boatman, played by the Common Man, but before he can embark, Cromwell butts in. He makes an excuse to question Thomas, to find out whether the meeting with the Cardinal has gone well: has Thomas agreed with Wolsey's strategy? Thomas indicates that he has not.

When Cromwell has left, the Spanish Ambassador Chapuys approaches. He too wants to know how Thomas will act concerning the divorce. Thomas refuses to cooperate, and Chapuys embarks on a tirade defending Queen Catherine and opposing any 'insult' to her. As he finishes, he too asks Thomas how he got on with the Cardinal, takes it from Thomas's reply that he did not support Wolsey's actions, and leaves well pleased.

More begins to realize what kind of pressures he is under, and travels home thoughtfully with the Boatman, chatting idly. As the scene ends, the Boatman slips back into character as Matthew the Steward.

The pull between various interests involved in the divorce has become obvious. Cromwell is shrewd, but as yet still subservient to Thomas. Chapuys surmises Thomas's support because he is emotionally convinced his cause is a just one. Thomas himself, though he maintains a tactful silence, begins to be worried by the situation, and to realize how wary he will need to be in order to be safe. He is nevertheless humanly interested in and sympathetic to the Boatman, who shows the Common Man's involvement in money, marriage and making a living.

Back home, More is surprised to find that William Roper is visiting Margaret. She tells her father that Will wants to marry her – and More immediately refuses. Will argues that he has just been appointed a barrister, but More (after congratulating the young man) says that he does not object to Roper's family or fortune, but to his beliefs, which are contrary to those of the Catholic Church.

Roper follows the views of Martin Luther. He criticizes the Church for charging for forgiveness of sins, and hints that for the proper price the Pope will also allow Henry's divorce. More challenges the gossip Roper has heard, begins to get angry at his attack on the Pope, and points out that Roper's views are always changing and are unstable. Finally he lends the young man a horse to get home and bids him goodnight.

Margaret questions Thomas about his meeting with Wolsey; he parries her remarks, but when she finally hints that the divorce question will lead to an attack on the Church, he warns her of the danger of her words.

Now Alice comes down. She too, after a tirade about Roper, questions More about Wolsey, but he refuses to discuss the matter. Alice then adds that Norfolk suggested that More should be Chancellor. More thinks that this is an unwise comment: Wolsey is still Chancellor and, if he were deposed, would take lesser men – like More – with him. The More family retire to bed.

Back with his family, Thomas is no less wary of speaking his mind. His reaction to Roper's proposal to Margaret shows us his firm Catholicism, but also allows us to see how he handles family crises. He is fond of Roper, but will not give way in something he believes harmful to his daughter, whom he loves. Margaret is not dominated by her father, but she does accept his judgement as final. Roper, a young man of high, but changeable principles, argues strongly but over-emotionally.

In the matter of the King's divorce, More shows the wariness which is part of his life. He defends the Church, and the Pope as divinely inspired, but will not discuss (or allow Margaret or Roper to discuss) anything that might be thought treasonable against his King. He is wary too at any suggestion of advancement: here is a man who, unlike most others in the play, is not ambitious.

The death of Cardinal Wolsey is both announced by the Common Man and symbolized by the bundling away of the Cardinal's hat and robe. We learn that Thomas More succeeded him, and was known as wise and good. This interlude shows us both the passage of time and events; from here on in the play, until the middle of Act Two, More is Chancellor.

A scenery change shows us that the location is Hampton Court. Cromwell meets Rich, who is now working for Norfolk and has come to Hampton Court with him. He parries Cromwell's questions about his exact employment but has to admit that he works in the library. Cromwell sneeringly compares their two situations, pointing out that Rich is the less important of the two even though he knows More, the Chancellor. At this point, Chapuys enters, and turns the conversation to what exactly Cromwell does; Cromwell says he is 'the King's Ear', the person who carries out the King's wishes: 'When the King wants something done, I do it' (p. 21). He gives as an example the launching of a new warship, the *Great Harry*. Cromwell has to arrange the King's piloting of the ship and his costume. Meanwhile, Cromwell waits – and gathers information for possible use later.

Chapuys replies sharply, correcting Cromwell's description of the ship, and reminding him that during the launch trip, Henry will visit More. Chapuys sees this as a sign of their friendship, Cromwell as the opposite: he knows Henry wishes to ask More again to change his mind about the divorce.

At this point the Steward enters. Both Cromwell and Chapuys expect the other to leave, so that they can approach the Steward for information. In the end Cromwell questions Matthew, while Chapuys partially hides.

The Steward tells Cromwell just what he wants to hear – that More is nervous about the divorce. Cromwell pays him and exits with Rich. Then the Steward stresses to Chapuys what *he* needs to hear – that More is a good and pious Catholic. The Steward allays Chapuys's suspicions about his talking also to Cromwell, and takes his money. Rich enters, eager to find out what Chapuys wanted. The Steward is honest with him, and when Rich leaves, explains his own philosophy; that he tells men what they want to hear, making them pay for and therefore value it even if it is common knowledge. He gloats over his coins as the scene changes.

This interaction between Cromwell and Chapuys highlights once again the opposing sides in the argument which will destroy More. The question of which is right is irrelevant; both think they are, and both believe that bribing a man to give information is not wrong in such circumstances. Even 'religious' Chapuys is short-sighted enough to believe the Common Man when he claims he serves God.

Cromwell's power has grown, and his hold on Rich is stronger. He brags of his rising power, and his unscrupulous methods are obvious. Chapuys is somewhat of a caricature, a too-holy diplomat taken in by flattery. Rich is beginning to waver; his position in Norfolk's household is not enough, and though resenting the implication that he will do so, he follows Cromwell. The Common Man, as Steward, shows even more of his weakness. He is the total opposite of More. He serves everyone, and has a shrewd grasp of human nature: although less educated, he is in many ways more intelligent than them. He is still suspicious of Rich.

The next scene is set in More's garden, on the day of the launching of the *Great Harry*. Alice, Norfolk and Meg are worriedly seeking Thomas, who should be there to greet the King. Norfolk forecasts that no good will come of More's attitudes, but Alice defends him stiffly. Meanwhile More appears, wearing a cassock from his daily attendance at church.

Norfolk is angry, while More is innocently surprised and defends his action: surely worshipping God is the best way to serve his office as Lord Chancellor? As the others pull off the cassock, then pull down his gown, he and they exclaim at each other. The furore is broken by the impressive entrance of the King, in gold. All kneel to him, and More welcomes him.

The King is in informal mood, excited by his river journey. He greets Alice, apologizing for the 'unexpectedness' of the visit. Although it has in fact been planned, it is supposed to be a surprise, so Alice stumbles over her reaction.

Next, the King is introduced to Margaret; her beauty makes him surprised she is a scholar, but she answers him shrewdly when he questions her in Latin about her teacher. In the end, her Latin is better than the King's, and he is put out: he speaks slightingly of learning, and then turns the conversation to an area in which he knows he excels – dancing. When Margaret admits she is not a good dancer, the King is back in a good humour and excitedly offers to beat Norfolk at wrestling. Seeing Norfolk is afraid for his dignity, Meg asks the King not to, and her gentleness meets with his approval. They talk about Henry's book on the Seven Sacraments, and Henry gets Meg to blow on his mock pilot's whistle to summon music from the players in his entourage.

This scene, with the family's panic, clearly demonstrates More's priorities. His individual response to God is more important than the pressures of society to conform and pay the correct honour to the King. Henry himself, in the only time he appears in the play, dominates everyone. We see his power, his kingship, in the way he rules; but we also see his impetuous immaturity in the way he needs to be best at everything. His attractiveness to women and the way he inspires loyalty in subjects such as Thomas are clearly shown.

The minor characters are also further revealed. Norfolk's reliance on form and ceremony, Alice's awe of high society, Meg's learning and gentleness, all add to our knowledge of them.

The family go in, and Henry and Thomas are left alone. Henry takes control of the conversation immediately, alternately listening to the music, talking of his steering of the ship, wishing he lived in the country, expecting More to respond, and then telling him to be silent and listen.

Then Henry mentions the Chancellorship: did More know that Wolsey suggested his appointment as Chancellor? More did not – and the mention of Wolsey sends Henry into a tirade against the Cardinal.

Henry thinks Wolsey failed in arranging the divorce because his ambition within the Church made him want to keep in the Pope's favour and not oppose him.

Suddenly, Henry changes the mood again, talking of his piloting of the ship, and just as suddenly switches back, asking More what his views on the divorce are now. More has to admit that he does not think the divorce is morally right. He would – literally, if the King wished – chop off his right arm in order to be able to agree with a clear conscience, but he cannot.

Henry is embarrassed. He sees More's real distress, remembers that he promised not to pressure More on this matter, and changes the subject. Almost immediately, though, the King returns with further argument. He says that his marriage to Catherine was illegal and immoral, that the original dispensation should not have been granted by the Church, and quotes from the Bible to prove his point. When Thomas counters with another quotation, Henry interrupts him, saying that the proof of the wrongness of his marriage is clear: he has no sons. It is his duty to divorce Catherine – for he is living in sin – and no one will stop him.

More wonders why the King needs his support. Henry replies that it is because More is honest. Others in the Court, like Norfolk, follow Henry because he is King, or, like Cromwell, because they want to benefit from him, or because they are a mindless mob. But More does none of these, and the King respects him.

He turns the talk again to lighter things – the music. More guesses, rightly, that the King composed the tune, and compliments Henry, who is pleased, and talks of staying for ever at Chelsea and living a life of ease. Just as quickly though, he is serious, warning Thomas harshly that he will have no opposition. He will leave Thomas out of the matter – but he will have his way; not even the Pope will make him live in sin, still married to Catherine. More, a little frightened, reassures the King that he will make no trouble, and Henry begs More to agree with him: 'You are the man I would soonest raise – yes, with my own hand' (p. 34). Eight o'clock strikes, and Henry at first suggests dinner, then decides he must leave. He bids goodbye to Thomas and to Alice, who has just entered, and leaves.

This is the focal point of Henry's visit, when he challenges More, using flattery, humour, persuasion, argument and threat, to try to make More agree. Henry's very real personal power shows through his kingly influence as well as his stubbornness and changeability. He seems genuinely concerned that he has sinned, yet needs More's backing in order to carry through the divorce.

More genuinely admires and respects the King, and is moved both by Henry's antagonism and support; but he says clearly what he feels to be right and will not move. His conscience is more important than both his fear of and love for Henry.

From this point on, we see Henry gradually, through Cromwell, reneging more and more on his promise not to pressurize More. We do not see the King again – the focus of interest is Thomas's reaction, not the King's – but we hear of his increasing discomfort at More's lack of support.

Alice now attacks Thomas for angering the King. At first apologetic, Thomas becomes irritated, but then realizes that Alice is anxious for him. He turns down her suggestion that he should try to manipulate the King into doing what he thinks best, but conversely he himself refuses to be manipulated by Henry. He reassures Alice that Henry has not gone early because he is angry, but rather because he wants to dance with Anne Boleyn; at this, Alice again shows her irritation that Thomas is preventing the divorce. More jokes with his wife that he may not submit to the King, but will certainly try to keep on the good side of him by flattery, but she is still uneasy. He tries to reassure her again by saying that he doesn't want to be a martyr.

This finale to the scene with Henry shows Alice's love for Thomas, her strong aggressive character and the power she has over him. But ultimately, Thomas will be manipulated neither by his King nor his wife.

Will Roper enters abruptly, followed by Margaret, who is trying to stop him. Roper says his conscience forces him in and, to More's amusement, Meg gives way.

Roper is worried. He has been offered a seat in the next Parliament (which would by inference mean supporting the King and his attitudes to Church reform). More comments that as Will is so in favour of reform, he could do well for himself. But Roper's views have changed (who foretold that they might do?). The attacks on the Church have made him realize how valuable it is, how inspired by God. He begins to speak harshly of those who criticize the Church, and Thomas – fearing Roper will say something treasonable which as Lord Chancellor he cannot listen to – tells him to be quiet. Roper accuses More of being too influenced by the Court, and of flattering to gain popularity, which is the direct opposite of Alice's recent charge.

At this point, Richard Rich enters. More's family, who know his true character, greet him cautiously. Roper, when he learns who Rich is, reacts suspiciously, and Rich is immediately on the defensive and makes to leave. Then he speaks quickly to More, warning him that Cromwell is collecting information about him; he even points out one of the sources – Matthew, More's Steward. More is unsurprised.

Rich appeals to More to help him – he is very distressed – but More will not employ him, because he does not trust him. Rich rushes out. Roper and Alice immediately suggest arresting Rich: they are afraid of him, and even Margaret feels he is a bad person.

But More points out that Rich has done nothing illegal, and therefore cannot be arrested. Roper contrasts the law of God, which Rich is breaking, with the law of Man, and accuses Thomas of being more respectful of Man's law than God's. More says that he isn't God. He can't decide what is right or wrong for other people; but he is clear about the law – and Rich has not broken the law.

Roper claims that in order to weed out moral wrongdoers, he'd break or abandon the laws, but More points out that the law is there to protect people, not just to punish. If there are no laws, even if they are abandoned for the best of reasons, then the wrongdoers can actually wreak havoc.

Roper fights back, saying More is too caught up in the law, while *he* conversely serves his God unswervingly. More retorts that he himself does serve God, but the country's laws protect him – and his daughter – which is more than Roper's ever-changing principles do. He storms out.

Margaret apologizes to Roper, who realizes something is wrong and asks what it is. Alice is upset because More did not refer to protecting her; Margaret comforts her. In a moment, Thomas returns and apologizes to Will, saying that in fact the lad's principles are fine. He suggests that they all start on the food prepared for, but uneaten by, the King.

Both Margaret and Alice, however, are still concerned. They question More about what is happening. He answers that he had not broken the law, and therefore is safe; the only reason that Cromwell is interested in him is that he is a prominent figure.

The family move to exit while More says a final word to Roper about principles – that he trusts Will but finds his ideals mutable. This is dangerous: principles are a stabilizing force, but Roper is changing them according to changing situations. Jovially, but with a serious note, More shows Roper the dangers of this.

This section of Act One, where both Rich and Will visit More, shows us firstly the net closing in around Thomas, and then his family beginning to become aware of it. We also get several insights into themes running through the play: good and evil, the law, and society and the individual. Roper's changing ideologies highlight for us the dangers of unanchored principles and contrast with Thomas's rock-steady morality. Rich is just as fickle as Roper, but is also evil – a fact realized by all. However, More draws a distinction between Rich's potential for wrongdoing and the fact that he has not broken the law. This, and More's exposition on the need for laws in a society, show us the distinction between law and morality.

We learn a little more about Roper in this section: he is changeable, but he is also genuine. Rich, on the other hand, is more and more unstable – this is his final cry for help before he loses his moral and political innocence to Cromwell in the next scene. Alice and Margaret are even more uneasy, while More, though worried, shows his basic commitment to and enthusiasm for his beliefs. We see here not the guilt of someone who cannot please his King, but the conviction of someone who knows he pleases his God.

The Common Man initiates a change of scene by hanging an inn sign on stage and altering his costume. The scene is an inn, called 'The Loyal Subject' (why do you think Bolt chose that name?) and he is its publican. He comments ironically that men as simple as he can't be expected to understand the deep thinking of Thomas More.

Cromwell enters, and greets the publican. The publican, who knows exactly who he is, denies doing so, which annoys Cromwell. He dismisses him with money. Then Cromwell calls in Rich, who is wary in case Cromwell is drunk. But Cromwell says he is only intoxicated by success; he has been appointed to the highly influential post of Secretary to the Council. Rich tries to hide his astonishment.

Cromwell turns the conversation to the topic of repeating or reporting information. Rich assures Cromwell that he is trustworthy, but Cromwell, far more worldly-wise than the other, queries this, pinning Rich down until he is forced to admit that in fact, if the price was right, he would repeat information. Cromwell congratulates him on his honesty in admitting this – and brushes aside Rich's naive assumption that 'there are *some* things one wouldn't do for anything' (p. 43).

Then Cromwell offers Rich an important post as Collector of Revenues for York Diocese. Rich immediately asks what the price is, and Cromwell answers that there is no price. Then he comments that everything comes down to convenience. Normally, if a man 'wants to change his woman' (p. 43), he can if it's convenient. When that man is King, however, then he changes his woman regardless, and the job of those like Cromwell is to make it convenient.

Cromwell breaks off to comment that Rich seems depressed, and Rich covers his mood by saying lightly that he has lost his innocence. What does he mean by this? Cromwell comments that More, conversely, is an innocent man and that this innocence, with its belief in the Church, is going to be an inconvenience to Henry's plans. It is the job of Cromwell and Rich to prevent this inconvenience.

Cromwell immediately begins to question Rich about the goblet More gave him – its worth, where More got it, the lawsuit for which it was a potential bribe. Rich replies, giving the information though he knows he is betraying More, and Cromwell congratulates him for that.

Rich challenges Cromwell about how he uses such information. When Cromwell replies that people like More have to be got out of the way somehow, Rich is critical, and defends Thomas. Cromwell says that More could be frightened, to which Rich replies that More doesn't know how to be.

To prove the point that fear is a powerful tool, Cromwell seizes

Rich's hand and puts it in the candle flame. The scene ends with Rich's horror at Cromwell's enjoyment of his pain.

This final scene of the Act leaves us on a note of foreboding, with Rich losing his innocence by betraying More to Cromwell, who now clearly states that he will stop More by whatever means it takes. The threat which has built up from the start of the play reaches a peak, leaving us genuinely shocked at Cromwell's final act of cruelty.

Rich himself is worried about what he is doing, and still protective of and defensive about More, whom he recognizes as a good man. We see Rich struggling with his conscience, hating Cromwell, yet drawn on by greed and a desire for power. Cromwell shows his willingness to do evil both by his actions towards Rich (and the publican) and by his attitude towards affairs of state in general and the divorce in particular. He is clever: he plays Rich like a fish, alternately encouraging and frightening him so that he gets what he wants.

Both men abandon moral principles – Cromwell actually hopes that Rich isn't religious – and, by inference, they abandon legal constraints also, in order to placate the King and run the country conveniently. They are both examples of the individual being corrupted by society – and in this scene, they join forces to become doubly dangerous.

ACT TWO

Act Two, like Act One, begins with the Common Man, who links the Acts and marks the passage of time. Two years have gone by, and Henry has put forward an Act of Parliament to establish the Church of England, of which he will be the head. If the Bill goes through, he will be able to grant his own divorce.

The lights go up to reveal More and Roper. Thomas queries the fact that Roper is dressed soberly, with a cross, and when Roper declares that he is showing his loyalty to the Church, More points out that Roper has changed. In turn, Roper criticizes the fact that, despite the King's actions, More still wears the Lord Chancellor's chain, a symbol of loyalty to the Crown. More, however, says he will not wear the chain if the Church of England is ratified by the Bishops. Roper thinks More is quibbling by waiting for the Bishops' verdict – surely the Act is contrary to Church beliefs – but Thomas points out that the Act's wording is 'so far as the law of God allows', and that *that* is a matter of opinion.

Roper asks More for his opinion, but Thomas will not give it, and warns Roper against expressing his view, which might be treasonable. He must not take risks, for he is now married to Margaret. Margaret enters, and learning what the talk is about, hopes that Roper will follow his conscience without thinking of his duty to her. More is concerned at her view.

The main point of this section is to show us the situation England and the Church are now in, and More's reaction to it. Roper has now changed his view to support the Church; More remains steadfast, loyal and cautious. We see from his warnings that he is very eager to remain safe, not to court danger or death – which makes his progress towards death even more courageous. As always, he uses the law as protection.

Now Chapuys enters; he overhears the family's talk and says that their defence of the Church makes them saintly. More teases Will about this, but is concerned about Chapuys inferring his own views. He will not state clearly to Chapuys what these are – and we are reminded why when a reference to his being called 'the English Socrates' makes More remember that that philosopher was executed.

More rebuffs Chapuys's overtures of friendliness, but asks the others to leave while he and the Ambassador talk business. They leave, exchanging Latin blessings with Chapuys, which makes More comment sarcastically on the 'holy language' of the Church.

Chapuys first reminds More that as Lord Chancellor he is partly responsible for Henry's actions in seeking a divorce and breaking from the Catholic Church. More is affected by this, and answers defensively. Chapuys admires More's actions but warns him that to give tacit approval now would be to corrupt himself. Chapuys has heard, however, that More will resign if matters go further.

More is relieved that Chapuys is not forcing him to choose openly between King and Church. He regains his composure and begins playing Chapuys at his own game, leading him into open approval of such a resignation, then to admission that factions in the country – in Yorkshire and Northumberland – would support More by force if necessary.

More's conversation with Chapuys shows not only his hostility towards the Spaniard's motives, but also his loyalty towards the King. Whatever More's views of Henry's attitudes to the Church, he protects him, using all his political skill to trap Chapuys into telling him where possible rebellion might start. Chapuys's defence of his religion raises our antagonism, while More's tongue-in-cheek view of the outward signs of Catholicism shows even more clearly that it is the inner belief which is important to him.

At this point, Roper enters to announce Norfolk. They obviously have news. Chapuys makes an excuse for being there and starts to leave, but stops to listen. Norfolk says that the Bishops have given in and broken the ties with Rome. Only Bishop Fisher argued against the break.

More realizes that at this point he cannot continue to be Chancellor. He goes to take off the chain of office, asking Norfolk to help him; Norfolk refuses. Roper offers a hand; More refuses this. He needs someone close to him to give him support. Alice responds with a tirade against More's action, to which More listens. Then he asks Margaret to help him, and she agrees.

Norfolk asks why Thomas is retreating from the situation; it seems cowardly. More replies that Henry's attack on the Church is not motivated by any desire to reform it, but is an act of personal vengeance because he cannot gain the divorce. Is the divorce correct, asks Norfolk, but More, knowing that to answer would be treason, will not say. He further defends his view by pointing out that the Pope may be corrupt but he is in direct line from the first Pope, and so divinely guided. This theory of Apostolic Succession may not be provable, but More believes it and must act accordingly.

Norfolk challenges Thomas to be clearer in what he says, but More knows that if he is, then Henry will use his words against him. Norfolk accuses him of a persecution complex: 'This isn't Spain you know' (p. 53). But More points out that if he did tell Norfolk his view on the divorce, Norfolk would have to tell the King or break his oath of obedience. Norfolk balks at the logic, calls More's words lawyer's tricks and says that he has no need to be afraid: the King accepts his resignation and will care for him as a loyal subject in future. More is not reassured.

As Norfolk turns to go, More stops him with a warning that there may be a Catholic rebellion in the North. Norfolk thanks him for the information, but says that it is already known – one of Cromwell's spies was secretly with Chapuys in the North. More is a little jealous that Cromwell has already acted on the matter. Norfolk leaves with a sarcastic comment that at least More had not entirely abandoned his loyalty; More responds angrily.

The announcement of the break with Rome pushes More one step further. In conscience, he cannot continue as Chancellor, giving tacit approval to the Act, so he must resign, doing what he thinks is right, uninfluenced by society and the antagonism of family and friends. He is still truly loyal to King and Country – but to God first.

Those around him react in varying ways. Norfolk, loyal to the King as a matter of duty and upbringing, cannot understand how More can put his religion first. He is frightened for him and therefore doubly angry, as is Alice, who sees her beloved husband giving up his position and all that goes with it. Roper, however, totally sides with More and supports him from now on. Here Margaret does too, though mainly because it is what her father wants. More reacts to them all with a mixture of kindness, impatience and intelligent argument; at bottom, however, he is increasingly motivated by both genuine fear and genuine courage.

More is left alone with his family. Alice is angry and More tries to calm her by painting a picture of happy seclusion. Roper congratulates Thomas warmly on his 'noble gesture', which worries Thomas, because what he has done is not simply a gesture, but a genuine response. The family scarcely understand what he is saying. Roper calls his action 'moral' (p. 55), as opposed to practical, which annoys More. Alice responds to More's accusation that their lack of understanding is cruel by saying it is he who is cruel, for behaving as he is, and she turns on Roper and Meg too. She warns More that the King will not simply leave him in peace.

More argues that he has made no treasonable statement; he has simply resigned. He is safe so long as he is silent. Alice responds that he is silent because he doesn't trust his family, but More points out that Alice can be made to talk, on peril of her soul, and that for all their sakes, it is better if they know nothing. At this point, the family begin to realize the dangers involved. Seeing this, More tries to cheer them up.

More's resignation of the Chancellorship finally brings home to his family the gravity of the situation. They all continue to react in their own way. More is first upset by their lack of understanding, but he cannot change his mind, and his love for them must come second to his love of God. When they realize the true danger, it is he who comforts them.

More and Alice are approached by Matthew, the Steward; the staff want to know what's happening. More says they will mostly have to go, but not before other jobs have been found for them. More asks Matthew if he will stay on. Matthew awkwardly says no, and More understands; he says he will miss the Steward.

Left alone, the Steward is thoughtful at More's kindness, but then angrily says that the comment is just a trick to get him to stay. He rants on resentfully that he's sorry for Sir Thomas, but everyone has bad luck. This little episode shows, after the reactions of nobility, friends and family, the reactions of the Common Man to More. When it comes to money, he won't support him, though he feels guilty. He reacts to More's kindness suspiciously, and doesn't understand it.

Action against Thomas is now under way. Norfolk and Cromwell are discussing him. Cromwell explains what effect Thomas's actions – even though he has made no declarations – are having on others, who see them as clear criticism. However, Thomas's warning to Norfolk of a possible Northern rebellion shows he is loyal, and Norfolk himself is convinced of this. Norfolk thinks that 'with a little pressure' (p. 58) Thomas can be persuaded to make a statement.

The pressure Cromwell has in mind is to get proof that Thomas accepted bribes; Norfolk is aghast: More is the most honest Chancellor ever. But Cromwell calls in Richard Rich and a woman. Rich has changed, become more confident – he greets Norfolk as a friend and is snubbed.

Cromwell turns his attention to the woman, Catherine Anger, who put forward a case in the Court of Requests in April 1526. Cromwell states that Thomas gave a correct judgement – but that shortly before the case, he accepted an expensive cup from the woman.

Norfolk thinks this is weak evidence, but Cromwell adds that the cup was later given to Rich, and that this can be proved by the evidence of More's Steward. Norfolk asks Rich when he received the cup – and then remembers that it was the night they both visited More in April 1526. It is obvious that 'the moment he knew it was a bribe he got rid of it' (p. 60). The case will not hold up in court.

Cromwell has to agree, hinting that they must find another way to entrap More. When Norfolk demurs, Cromwell threatens him by commenting that the King wants him involved. In that way it will be clear to the world that More is not being persecuted. Norfolk leaves, angrily.

Cromwell turns on Rich, blaming him for making the plot fail. Rich apologizes. Cromwell then hints that they must take further action against More. Rich is wary, but Cromwell reassures him that everything will be done 'legally', even if they have to create a new law for the occasion.

Cromwell is now starting to take direct action against Thomas. He will do anything – even twist the law – to persuade him to submit. Though controlled and effective, Cromwell is under more and more pressure.

Norfolk, forced to be involved, is confused. He backs the King because it is his duty and his inborn way of life. But he defends Thomas as his friend, and because he has a natural sense of justice.

Rich has changed. He is still wary of going too far, but he has more self-confidence, and we can see that he will do almost anything that is necessary. He is in awe of Cromwell, but tries to be equal to Norfolk – to the latter's fury.

The Steward asks Rich for a post. Rich, remembering Matthew's previous attitude to him, shrilly rebukes him, using his new-found power. But Matthew subtly flatters him into employing him. Now he is in a position of power, Rich uses it – but the Common Man is still able to manipulate him.

The scene changes to More's house, where the loss of his post is beginning to show in the family's poverty. Chapuys and his attendant have just arrived and Alice, obviously now acting as housewife, is warning them to leave.

Left alone, Chapuys and the attendant discuss how More's situation has changed and how he is suffering. Chapuys praises Thomas, though he warns his attendant not to *like* the ex-Chancellor. Chapuys, echoing Cromwell's words on p. 58, is sure that More supports his side, simply because he is opposed to the other.

When More appears, Chapuys tries to give him a letter from the King of Spain, but More refuses to touch it. Chapuys praises More for 'taking a stand' on the divorce, but Thomas points out that no one actually knows his views, and that to accept the letter would immediately put him in danger of being thought to side with Spain. He would have to take the letter straight to the King.

At this point, Meg enters; she has been collecting bracken for the fire, to More's approval. He asks her and Alice to witness that he has neither read nor accepted the letter from Spain, and then subtly dismisses Chapuys, who leaves coldly, feeling snubbed, with the comment, 'The man's utterly unreliable' (p. 64).

More will not bend to Cromwell, nor will he side with Chapuys. You may like to consider what More's real position is: is there a third alternative for him?

He is careful both to remain loyal to the King and to protect himself legally by having witnesses to his loyalty. Chapuys expects Thomas to side with him politically, just because he is still a loyal Catholic; but Thomas does not mix the two issues and thus incurs Chapuys's displeasure.

The state of the More family is clearly shown, in practical details such as the bracken, and in Alice's attitude, which is defensive and angry. More takes to poverty well, because he has his principles to cling to.

Alice, Meg and More discuss their situation. Alice is weary of poverty and reacts badly both to More's jokes about it and to his attempts to philosophize: 'We could be beggars and still ... be merry together' (p. 65). More, who has been offered money by the Bishops, explains that he cannot take it because to be paid by the Church would imply that he supported it, and if Henry continues to harass him, it could turn 'bad'.

Alice queries the word 'bad' (More actually means treasonable, punishable by death) and More reassures her, but at that moment Will Roper enters. More has been summoned to appear before Cromwell to answer charges. The family is shocked. More tries, unsuccessfully, to appear unconcerned, and comforts first Alice, then Margaret, who wants to come with him. He jokes about bringing Cromwell back to their meagre dinner, and both Meg and Roper tell More not to joke about such things; but Thomas replies that Cromwell is not someone to be afraid of.

Thomas's situation is made even more clear by the comments of his family. They love him, but still do not understand his position, and their lack of understanding as well as their poverty grieves him. He cannot explain the true situation to them, and does not want to worry them by admitting that he may be in danger. Notice his contempt for Cromwell, and his belief, later disproved, that because his case is legally watertight, he is safe.

The scene changes; More is at Hampton Court facing Cromwell and Rich. More greets Rich kindly, noticing his affluence. Cromwell tries to establish a relaxed atmosphere by telling Thomas he admires him, but Thomas comes straight to the point and asks what the charges are. Cromwell merely wants to clarify why Thomas is opposed to 'the whole movement of the times' (p. 67). The King is displeased with More, but would offer him anything if he would give his support. More replies coolly, so Cromwell continues to pressurize him, by mentioning the 'Holy Maid of Kent', whom Thomas once met and talked with. Thomas agrees that he sympathized with her fate, but will not admit to agreeing with her. Cromwell is sure that when they talked, the Maid must have made a treasonable statement; yet More did not report this, which is also treasonable. More says he has witnesses not only to the conversation but also to a letter he wrote her. Cromwell has to back down.

Next, Cromwell speaks of the book *A Defence of the Seven Sacraments*, which Henry wrote. More comments bitterly that Henry was commended by the Pope for the book – which leads to a discussion of the Pope's authority. Knowing that to comment on the power of the Pope over the Church of England may lead him into treasonable statements, More slyly refers Cromwell back to the King's book.

Cromwell then accuses More of writing the book, which Thomas denies. He only answered certain questions Henry asked him. Henry knows this, and will not give contrary evidence. When Cromwell queries this, Thomas replies that Henry certainly will not perjure himself. He is a man who will tell the truth as he sees it and Cromwell ought to know the King better than to think otherwise.

Stopped on two counts, Cromwell finally turns to the crux of the matter: he asks Thomas directly what his opinion is of Henry's marriage to Anne. Thomas is taken aback. Henry had promised not to ask him this again. Then Cromwell announces that the King now thinks Thomas to be a villain and a traitor. Thomas realizes, probably for the first time, that the law is not enough protection – he is the victim of the King's displeasure. 'So I am brought here at last' (p. 69). Cromwell points out that it is More's own actions which have brought him to his current position, but More adds that other people are responsible too. Cromwell lets him go.

Cromwell adds after he has gone that More is a man who makes trouble but will not face the consequences. He tells Rich that they will not be able to frighten More into submission; so if Thomas will not approve of the marriage, he must be destroyed. The King, it seems, is a man of conscience – and can talk himself into believing that if he destroys someone, that person deserves to be destroyed. Rich is shaken by this. Cromwell adds that the King's conscience seems never to be satisfied.

This is the first formal attack by Cromwell on More. He is bright, cunning and ruthless. He will do whatever is necessary to please the King and thus better himself. More parries all Cromwell's moves effectively, though he becomes more and more aware of the danger he is in. The two are well matched in intelligence and strength of character. Notice how skilfully More argues his legal case, but also how affected he is when, finally, he realizes the King's change of heart.

For Cromwell, this meeting removes the possibility that he can pressure More with words, and he realizes he will have to use sterner measures. Rich is wary but goes along with what is happening. Even though he is not present, we are constantly kept aware, by references to him, of the King's influence over what is happening.

Returning home, More calls for a boat, but none of the boatmen will take him. Norfolk enters and More, realizing that he is now a marked man, thanks his friend for being seen with him. Norfolk berates Thomas for his stupid behaviour, pleading that, even if only for his friend's sake, he should submit, and warns More that the King is using him (Norfolk) in his plans. More replies that if he is dangerous to know, then Norfolk should break off the friendship with him. Norfolk says this is impossible: they like each other, so the answer is for More to give in. More replies that this too is impossible; friendship is important to him, but his beliefs and his God are the very centre of his being.

Norfolk pleads with More. More is moved, but prefers to end the friendship there. Norfolk will not listen – he does not want to lose Thomas – but More deliberately begins to pick a quarrel.

Norfolk at first refuses to be drawn but, as More insults his religious commitment, then calls their friendship merely the result of laziness, he begins to be angry. Thomas speaks of the dogs Norfolk breeds – water spaniels, whose very essence is to have a liking for water. Just so, Thomas's very essence opposes the King's wish – not because of what he wants, but because of what he is. But he wonders if Norfolk has that essence; if he does, he needs to give it some exercise, for at present Norfolk is merely giving in to what he wants. He is in no fit state to meet God – in fact, his line seems morally tainted. Norfolk is highly insulted by this, and goes to hit Thomas, who ducks. Norfolk rushes off, and More is left regretfully looking after him.

More deliberately cuts himself off from his friend Norfolk – for Norfolk's sake. He hates doing so, but he is able to put his personal needs second to his friend's safety. Norfolk is genuinely fond of More, but his temper and pride overrule this, and, on his side, the friendship does not stand the test. More has to put friendship second to his conscience; Norfolk's conscience is second to his inbred need to conform, to obey the King.

Meg and Roper enter, and break the news that an Act concerning the marriage is being put through Parliament: everyone has to take an oath, or else be charged with treason. More is immediately concerned, but hopes that he can legally escape the oath. He counters Roper's comment that the wording of an oath is unimportant by saying that, on the contrary, the wording may make it possible to escape. Aware that Roper thinks he is just bandying words, More adds that in such logical complexity, such mind games, man serves God best. In some situations, there is no escape, but in others, man's mind can save him and glorify God at the same time.

The final section of the scene, where More learns about the oath, is the turning-point for him. After this, he is imprisoned. He rests his confidence in the law. He sees man – himself, in fact – as glorious in mental capacity, particularly in the 'tangle' of his mind, manifested, for instance, in legal argument. Notice More's attitude to God, whom he speaks of as another person, who has control over mankind, but who can still be 'delighted' (p. 74).

The scene changes to show a dungeon and instruments of torture. The Common Man is now the Jailer; he says it is a job like any other, but more distasteful than most. He points to More in the cage, and says he wishes he could let him out – but this would mean taking his place.

The Common Man then indicates Cromwell, Norfolk, Cranmer and Rich, and tells the audience what their fates were: Cromwell was executed for treason, Norfolk was saved from a similar end by the King's death of syphilis, Cranmer was burned alive – and Rich became Lord Chancellor and died in his bed.

This little interlude begins the section of the play leading to More's death. Why do you think Bolt includes at this point an account of how other characters died?

More is now in jail, for not taking the oath. The Jailer rouses him – it is one o'clock in the morning – and leads him before the tribunal. Norfolk announces the start of the inquiry, and Cromwell checks that the witnesses are present. Then Cromwell shows More the Act of Succession and the names of those who have taken the oath. More refuses to sign it, obviously not for the first time. Norfolk begins to question Thomas, to Cromwell's annoyance.

More explains that he is quite willing to recognize Queen Anne's children as heirs to the King, but will not swear to the oath. Norfolk, slow on the uptake as usual, wonders why; there is more in the Act than simply recognizing Anne's children as heirs, replies Cromwell. The tension between the two is such that Cranmer takes over the questioning. He states that the Act claims that Henry's marriage to Catherine was unlawful; does More agree? More refuses to reply. Norfolk chides him, then says that More's reasons for not taking the oath must be treasonable. Not necessarily, says Thomas: they have no actual proof, nor do they know for sure that Thomas objects to the Act; they only know that he will not swear. This is vital. For simply not swearing, Thomas has been imprisoned and impoverished. If he has treasonable reasons for not swearing, however, he can be executed.

Norfolk understands all this, with difficulty. He does, however, appeal to Thomas, 'for fellowship' (p. 78), to agree with all those who have taken the oath. Thomas asks whether, if he goes to hell for not following his conscience, Norfolk will come with him 'for fellowship'.

Cranmer wonders if everyone who took the oath will go to hell. More replies that taking the oath is a matter of conscience: everyone must make his own decision. If Thomas thinks the matter is uncertain, says Cranmer, he should sign, for there is no uncertainty about his duty to the King. Thomas replies that the King cannot alter what is or is not, even if men have different views on it. More will not sign. Cromwell, trying to trick More into admitting his reasons, asks on what grounds he will not, but More evades the question. Cromwell then threatens him, and More rebukes him for not being just – Thomas has no fear, as long as he is being dealt with justly. Just before going back to his cell, More asks for more books; Cromwell viciously refuses him permission to have any, or to see his family, and More exits.

More's situation is now serious, though he does not yet realize that the law he trusts in will not protect him when it is wielded by Cromwell. Once again we see how his religion triumphs; he sincerely believes that if he perjures himself, he will be eternally damned, and against this, his loyalty to the King is nothing. Here we also begin to see Thomas's physical deterioration. He becomes more vulnerable, though never swayed.

Cromwell is impatient and constantly irritated by Norfolk and his slow, good-natured plodding. Cranmer, in title a Bishop, seems to have little spirituality.

When More has gone, Cromwell questions the Jailer, making him promise on oath to report any significant remarks made by More. He also promises him fifty guineas for information, which scares the Jailer – anything worth so much money is dangerous. This episode shows the Common Man's reactions to More's situation: he won't stop it, but neither will he become too involved.

Cromwell orders Rich to remove More's books the next day and Norfolk queries the necessity of this, but Cromwell replies that it must be done and that the King is getting impatient.

When Norfolk and Cranmer exit, Rich approaches Cromwell and asks for the vacant post of Attorney-General for Wales. Cromwell brushes him aside. He is worried; the King is uneasy, for Thomas is a constant reproach to him. But if More is executed, Cromwell is sure his own death will follow. So More must submit. Cromwell turns to the rack, but knows the King will not allow torture. What can he do?

The reactions of the Commission to one another and to More are shown here – Norfolk's soft-heartedness, Rich's selfishness, Cromwell's concentration on the job in hand. Details in this section – the mention of the post of Attorney-General, Rich's order to collect the books – are important later in the play. How?

The Jailer announces to More a visit from his family, then reassures him that they are not themselves imprisoned. He lets More out of his cage, and Thomas greets first Meg, then Alice and Roper. More's family is horrified at the jail, but Thomas reassures them it is not too bad. He is delighted with the food they bring, but soon starts to question why his family is here. Roper begs More to swear to the Act, and then reveals that Meg is under oath to persuade him to do so. More is displeased, and upset that she should want him to betray his principles.

But Meg argues with her father in order to save his life. Her first attempt is to suggest that Thomas say the words of the oath out loud, but actually think what he believes. More counters this successfully by saying that the whole point of an oath is that we are saying the words of it to God, and adds that taking an oath is like holding one's self like water in one's hands: to lie is to betray one's very self. More cannot be anything but honest when he takes an oath.

Meg is convinced by this, but has another argument. Isn't Thomas proudly making himself a hero by his actions? Thomas replies that if the State was a good one, everyone would be a good person, and there would be no need for heroes; but doing bad things actually gets more rewards than doing good, so despite the pride involved in setting oneself up as a hero, maybe sometimes we have to choose to do good things in order to contradict what is happening in society.

Finally, Meg makes an emotional appeal directly to Thomas – hasn't he done enough? Alice joins her as they tell More how terrible life at home is without him. At this, he begins to break, accusing Meg of torturing him by her words.

Thomas has had to face pressure from the King, Norfolk, Cromwell and society in general; now his family tries to persuade him to change his mind. He still holds firm, meeting every argument intelligently, logically and with a firm conscience, even though he is terribly swayed both by the sight of his family and by hearing how they fare. Meg loves her father. That is why she tries to pressurize him, but at bottom she can only understand intellectually what he is doing.

At this point, the Jailer enters, telling More that the family must leave in only two minutes. Thomas is panic-stricken, and instructs Roper to delay the Jailer by drinking and playing dice with him. Roper agrees eagerly.

Then More turns to Meg and Alice, instructing them to flee England, even if it means leaving him. Meg agrees. Alice is angry, and More tries to win her round by complimenting her on her cooking and her appearance.

Alice rebukes him for patronizing her, and More then tries to speak to his wife honestly. He tells her that he is very afraid of death, but even more of dying without her understanding why he has to do so.

But Alice cannot understand. She thinks More could have avoided the situation, and she is afraid that she will hate him for choosing death. More is devastated and breaks down – and at this, Alice goes to him, and they hold each other. She knows he is 'the best man that I ever met' (p. 86) and, in this moment, accepts that if he dies it is God's will. And she will defend him against the King and Council, whatever it costs.

More comes alive again: 'Why, it's a lion I married!' (p. 86). He is proud of Alice, and content now to accept whatever happens because she accepts it. Then, overcome by grief, he breaks down.

In the middle of this, the Jailer rushes in, realizing that Roper is trying to delay him. More argues, Meg pleads, Alice is fighting mad – but as seven o'clock strikes, the Jailer has his way. He hurries Meg and Roper out, and forces Alice up the stairs, who berates him all the way. As she turns to go, More calls a last, loving goodbye. The Jailer, uncomfortable at his actions, apologizes to More.

This scene with Alice crystallizes what we know of More as a family man. He deeply loves Alice and depends on her. Alice is not as intelligent as More – unlike Meg, she cannot begin to understand what he is doing – but she loves him and trusts him and God to do what must be done. This support is what More needs to carry him through.

This scene contains some of the most deeply emotional parts of the play, where we see what suffering More's actions really caused him, and see him as very human and very vulnerable.

The scene changes to a courtroom. The Common Man helps More to the Accused's chair, and then arranges chairs for the jury. The people he has previously played – Steward, Boatman, Innkeeper and Jailer – are represented on the jury, and he himself is challenged by Cromwell to be the Foreman. In the meantime Cromwell announces in formal and ringing verse that English law is about to be brought into action. He likens it to a ship; and during this court case, 'quicksands' (p. 89), where the law may falter, will be identified and charted.

This change of scene begins the climax of the play. We see the formal panoply of law (which is about to be totally misused) set up and honoured. We also see both nobles and the Common Man involved in the process.

Norfolk opens the case by announcing that Thomas is accused of high treason, but may obtain pardon from the King if he repents. More replies steadfastly, calling on God for mercy and apologizing for his weak state of health.

Next, Cromwell reads the charge, prefacing it with a reference to the fact that More's friend Bishop Fisher has been executed that morning; as calculated, this shocks More deeply. The charge is of denying that the King is head of the Church. More is indignant at this, for he has never denied it, merely refused to take the oath. Cromwell and Norfolk repeat to More that he is here on a charge of high treason, which is punishable by death. More responds that everyone dies – even kings. Norfolk, concerned, tells More that he can avoid death, but Thomas answers that he will not do so; Christ himself went willingly to his end, and so should all men.

This first section of the trial reminds us of the issues: More has not taken the oath, but has not said anything treasonable. We see him now totally surrounded by enemies and yet at ease, almost as if ready to die. He is just starting to realize that the trial may have been rigged.

The case begins. Thomas's claim that he has committed no crime by being silent is challenged. Cromwell says there are many kinds of silence. There are, for instance, the silence of the dead and the silence which allows violence to happen without stopping it. More refused to take the oath and kept silent on the matter. But, Cromwell claims, this lets everyone know that More disagrees with the oath – it is actually denial, and so treasonable.

More immediately argues that the maxim of the law is 'Silence Gives Consent'. No one knows why he will not take the oath, but on these grounds, they must assume that he consents to it. Cromwell begins to be angry and accuses More of clouding the issue. More retorts that it is not a question of issues, but of keeping within the law. If someone is within the law, as More is, he should be safe.

Also, a 'loyal subject' (p. 92) should follow his conscience, which is more important than anything, and necessary in order to save his own soul. Cromwell here angrily accuses More of wanting to protect not his eternal soul, but his own life, his own conceit, and of forgetting that he has a duty to the King. But More responds that a liar can be of no use to the King, and he would have to be a liar to take the oath.

In this section, Cromwell argues with More about the meaning of More's silence. We see justice perverted and arguments used falsely. More defends the law and its place, and the right of a man to follow his conscience; he is frightened but in control. Cromwell, increasingly angry, argues that conscience is just self-indulgence. From this point on we see clearly his vicious desire to destroy More.

Stung, Cromwell calls Rich to give evidence. He appears, obviously now wealthy and influential, and takes the oath (notice how he 'forgets' the reference to God). Then Cromwell questions him, and Rich declares that on 12 March he visited More in prison to remove his books. During their conversation, they discussed what power Acts of Parliament had, and agreed that they could create Rich as King, but could not uncreate God as God. Then, Rich claims, More said clearly that an Act of Parliament could not make the King head of the Church – he denied the title.

More realizes at this point that he is lost, because of Rich's perjury. He first responds with typical compassion, worried for Rich's eternal soul. Then he argues Rich's claim and swears on oath that he did not deny the title. Why should he do so after keeping silent for so long? He remembers too that there were other witnesses, Southwell and Palmer; Cromwell explains that both are out of the country, and in any case have given evidence that they did not hear a word. Thomas tries to argue that, had he really denied the title, the importance of that would have made Rich immediately call Southwell and Palmer as witnesses.

Now, however, as More says, he is 'a dead man' (p. 95). He warns Cromwell that by persecuting him for what he believes, Cromwell will make other men deny what they believe, out of fear, and soon 'they will have no hearts' (p. 95).

Before Rich leaves, More calls to him; he examines the chain of office Rich wears, and learns that the man is now Attorney-General for Wales. More is sad that Rich should have lost eternal life for such a pitiful reward.

At this point, Cromwell turns to Thomas to offer him the King's mercy. To gain this, however, More would have to take the oath. He refuses.

Norfolk tells the jury to consider the evidence. Cromwell thinks that it should not be necessary, and indeed, when asked, the Foreman immediately returns a verdict of guilty. Norfolk begins to read the sentence.

Rich has given evidence, perjured himself and condemned More. We know that More will die, so this is no surprise, but it is nevertheless a dramatic climax. More is trapped; he fights with argument, but has to lose. He is resigned, while being sorry that Rich has done what More has fought so hard not to do – damned himself. Rich goes through with the perjury. Unlike Cromwell, however, he is not triumphant with what happens; he is defensive and ashamed.

Norfolk is fooled by Rich. He has, throughout, followed the letter of the law, accepting that it is just even when its course has been perverted. It is he who conducts the formalities and ultimately reads the sentence. The law, ultimately, is proved to be corruptible.

More interrupts. Now his fate is sealed, he can allow himself what he wants – a chance to speak out. He demands the right to make a statement. Clearly, he condemns the King; the King cannot be head of the Church, for that is a title to be bestowed by God alone. The King should not attack the Church: this is contrary both to the Magna Carta of England and the King's own Coronation Oath.

More adds that he has been loyal to King and Country, and he is a good man. If this is not enough to live, he is happy to die – indeed, several times since he has been in prison, he has been close to death and content with that. He adds, finally, that although he has been condemned on the issue of the King's Supremacy, in fact it is because he disagrees with the marriage that he must die.

More's long final speech states his real position fully for the first time. He no longer has anything to lose, so he speaks out against the King, the Act and the break with the Church. The speech shows his goodness, intelligence, holiness – and real spirit. These were More's actual words in the trial, affirming his love of God and loyalty to the King.

Norfolk pronounces sentence – that More has been found guilty of high treason and is to be beheaded. Immediately the scene changes; the court scenery disappears, an axe and block are shown silhouetted, and three spotlights appear, to the left and right and on the arch.

Cromwell now orders the Common Man to take the part of the Executioner which, after demurring, he does, using a mask which Cromwell gives him.

Events move swifly towards their inevitable conclusion. Norfolk offers wine to Thomas, which he refuses; Norfolk has betrayed his friend, and is not strong enough to go with him. Meg emotionally runs to More, but he comforts her and then steps aside. The woman who tried to bribe More stops him; he repeats that his judgement on her case was a correct one, and goes quickly towards the block. Finally, he is followed by Cranmer, whom he tells to turn back. Thomas reaches the block alone and reassures the Headsman, 'You send me to God.' He is sure of that, for he knows God will not reject someone who has so willingly followed the road to heaven.

The drums roar, the lights dim, and all exit. From the darkness, the Headsman calls out the traditional proclamation, 'Behold the head of a traitor' (p. 99).

The actions immediately preceding More's death are stylized, and remind us of Jesus's procession to death, approached first by one person, then another. The parallels with Christ are clear: More too is dying for what he believes in and for his love of God. He resolves everything, freeing himself from family and friends, keeping his sense of justice to the last, able to forgive the Headsman and sure of his welcome in heaven.

There are two alternative endings to the play. In the first, Cromwell and Chapuys enter together, at first hostile, then recognizing that they are both the same – worldly-wise survivors. They exit together.

In the second ending, the Common Man comes forward for a final speech to remind us that, unlike Thomas More, we are still alive. To remain alive, it is only necessary not to make trouble. Finally, he asks us to recognize him when we meet him.

The alternative endings stress different aspects of the play. In one, the opposing factions who have warred over More join together, realizing that their ends are the same. They are the survivors because they compromise; More is a martyr because he does not.

The Common Man points out further the relevance of the play to the audience. We are still alive, unlike More; we should avoid making trouble, unlike him. And we should remember too that the Common Man is everywhere – and recognize him when we meet him.

Characters

WOMAN

Catherine Anger is the woman who tries to bribe More by giving him a goblet. She was in the wrong, but thinks she can affect justice with money. We meet her when she is called to give evidence to Cromwell (p. 59) and she appears briefly just before More's death (p. 98). She is shown as vindictive and corrupt, but her character in itself is not important.

Her significance in the play is that, because of her, we see More's incorruptibility and devotion to the right use of the law. Even Cromwell states that his handling of the woman's case was correct. The bribery issue seems a threat to More, as Cromwell tries to use it to put pressure on the Chancellor. In fact More triumphs, showing in his attitude to the affair even just before he dies that he knows what is right and keeps to it.

ARCHBISHOP CRANMER

There are two churchmen in the play, Cranmer and Wolsey. Cranmer is appointed to his post after the split with Rome and therefore is an Archbishop of the Church of England.

We learn very little about his character. He is described as lacking 'religiosity' and as being 'sharp-minded' (p. xxiv). On the occasions we meet him – the questioning of Thomas while in jail (p. 75ff.), administering the oath to Rich during the trial (p. 93) and just before Thomas's execution (p. 99) – we learn little about him. We see in him, as presented in the play, a man for whom the issues of whether the split was correct, or whether Henry is the head of the new Church, are not important. Cranmer is not a religious man, devoted to his faith (he scarcely mentions God throughout); he is an administrator, who carries out his King's orders. He seems unvindictive, almost gentle with Thomas, and although sharp, can bring forward no real arguments against him.

Cranmer is included in the play not only because he was an actual historical person, present at the events described. Though undeveloped, his character represents one view of religion; he is a churchman of the time. He contrasts with the immoral Cardinal Wolsey, and represents Anglican as opposed to Catholic religion. He also, more importantly, makes us see that even as a churchman he is not as truly good as More, a layman. In the end, he seems almost jealous of Thomas's certainty that he will go to heaven – a certainty we share.

ALICE

Thomas's wife is almost the direct opposite to her husband, an uneducated woman of the merchant class who has little wariness or circumspection and who cannot really understand her husband's actions.

Alice appears at regular intervals throughout the play, and we gradually build up a picture of a good housewife and mother, with much common sense but no intellectual power. Her world is at home. She has come up in life and can scarcely handle her situation. She is overdressed, with none of the subtleties of the nobly born such as Norfolk. She 'worships' society, and is stung when, in Act Two, Thomas gives up the Chancellorship and she loses her place in the world.

Consistently throughout the play, Alice is seen as strong-willed. She argues with Norfolk over the falcon (p. 5), frets at More to look after himself, stands up to Chapuys. We may see this behaviour as a real threat to her relationship with More, for she is genuinely angry at his stand and resists his progress towards martyrdom all the way. He is very distressed at her reaction.

However, Alice's anger is in fact proof of her love for More. She 'worships' him (p. xxiii), and because she does not understand what he is doing, sees only her beloved husband losing all for an ideal, and so tries to stop him. More himself suffers most of all because of this: he willingly breaks friendship with Norfolk over his stand, but is closest to giving in when Alice does not support him. In the end, however, Alice accepts what Thomas is doing, and in a truly moving scene, declares her love for 'the best man that I ever met' (p. 86). Thus strengthened, More can do what he knows is right. We see Alice's very real courage here in defending him; she is even prepared to speak out for him before the King at risk of her life (p. 86).

Is Alice a 'good' woman? Undoubtedly. Her religion is not deep and thoughtful, but straightforward and uncomplicated; she trusts a God who 'knows why' things happen. Her behaviour is not saintly, but often uncharitable, rough and cruel. But Alice is brave and kind-hearted, and possesses a strength of character which, like More's, is untouched by the pressures of convention and people around her; her religion, like More's, is as essential and natural to her as breathing.

The presence of Alice in the play is concrete proof of More's humanity; an academic, a philosopher, a saint, he still has a warm, loving, vibrant relationship with his wife. It is not an easy relationship – which in itself proves his humanity, his vulnerability. Its emotional strength contrasts sharply with the intellectual argument we find elsewhere in the play, and shows us clearly what More is giving up by choosing the path he does.

MARGARET

Margaret (Meg), Thomas More's daughter, is young, attractive, intelligent and educated – almost too much so for her time, it appears. She is sensitive and aware, able to attract the King without flirting with him, able to enjoy jokes while not wanting to see Norfolk humiliated.

As with all characters in the play, it is Meg's relationship with More which is of central importance. She comforts her mother, defends Roper and stands up to the King, but it is to More that she relates most subtly. They have an obvious deep affection for each other, which on her side is marked by respect and obedience – she accepts More's judgement on her marriage with Roper – but is nevertheless an equal one. She is not dominated by More, but has been raised by him to be educated, analytical and his match. It is she, of all the family, who supports More by taking off his Chancellor's chain when he resigns.

So, when More is in prison, it is Margaret who comes to him and tries to persuade him to take the oath. More is displeased with her for attempting to make him waver, but she is following her conscience as much as he is, 'I wanted to!' (p. 83). The arguments she puts forward are clear and logical, and we discover a great deal through them, not only about More's shrewdness and wit, but about Margaret's intelligence, and the way she has been well trained by her father.

But in the end, More will not budge, and Margaret has to resort to emotional pleas, which do move him. And it is here – as with Alice – that Margaret's role in the play becomes clear: she shows us More as a family man, vulnerable because he loves.

Meg, like many of those in the play, is not fully developed as a character. Her importance is in what she shows us of More. Notice how it is she, not Alice (to whom More has already said goodbye), who greets Thomas on his way to execution. Laying aside her logic, she calls to him from the heart, and he in turn holds her, but leaves her. In the final analysis, Meg shows us that More's fate takes precedence over his family.

WILL ROPER

One of Thomas More's main characteristics is his steadfastness: he holds rock-steady principles despite social pressure, poverty, imprisonment and death. Contrasting with this, and therefore highlighting

More's personality, is Will Roper, whose changeability dominates his character.

Will Roper is a lawyer, of a good family, who rises during the course of the play to become a Member of Parliament. He is intelligent, educated and affluent. From what we know of him, he is kind-natured, perhaps a little too serious for his own good, and strong-willed. All of these characteristics endear him both to More – who likes and respects him – and to Meg, who returns his love.

The weakness in all this is Will's changeability. He has a passion for religion: at the start of the play we see a rabid Lutheran, then later a devout Catholic. For both religions, he is outwardly and dangerously ready to be a martyr. He can change his beliefs. They are not steadfast, because his passion alters what he feels from one side to the other with equal abandon. More is always worried by this ('I'd trust you with my life ... but not your principles' (p. 41)), for he himself loves God simply, quietly and consistently. It is this contrast which makes Will's place in the play so valuable, for it allows us to see More's stable goodness.

Their relationship is stormy. We first see Will when More firmly, if kindly, refuses him permission to marry Meg. Then, after the King's visit, Roper's arrival leads to an argument with More about the place of the law. Again we learn, by contrast, how valuable More's view is when compared to Will's anarchism. Will, in turn, thinks More hypocritical, a flatterer who will not risk himself for his God, who puts the law before morality.

In the end, of course, More does act for what he believes, and from this point on, Will is totally on his side. He is genuinely moved by what has happened and offers to remove More's chain of office when he resigns from the Chancellorship. Once the two men are, in this way, reconciled, Roper loses his main role in the play, and appears only briefly, in the jail, as a supportive part of More's family.

Cromwell, Wolsey, Cranmer – all offer contrasts to More and all are judged wrong. Roper is not. In some ways, he is even like More. He follows his conscience, and is at bottom a good man. His principles are strong, and he is prepared to follow them to their conclusion. However, in the main, the differences between Will and More are Roper's main contribution to the play.

WOLSEY

Wolsey, like Cranmer, is a Church leader, but of the Catholic not the English Church. We meet him only briefly in the first part of Act One. Historically, he tried and failed to gain Henry's divorce, and died on his way to be tried for treason.

Robert Bolt's Wolsey is a corrupt but shrewd churchman. He is worldly, political, in love with power. He fights to maintain his position as Lord Chancellor, by doing exactly what the King wants (despite his contempt for Henry). In addition, we feel that he genuinely fears the wars that may result from an England without an heir: he, unlike Thomas, does not let his 'own, private conscience' (p. 12) get in the way when politics is involved.

Wolsey is Thomas's superior, the only person in the play, except the King, to whom Thomas defers, at least on the surface. Wolsey admires Thomas, but is impatient with his real holiness, his simple goodness, which seems to him to be both naive and ineffectual. He alternately tries to bully, persuade, argue and trap More into supporting him, but ultimately fails.

Although appearing only briefly, the Cardinal is important. His conversation with More sets the scene for us, outlining the issues and laying the basis for the main action of the play. His character, so unlike More's, lets us see from the start what sort of person More is. Unlike the Cardinal, he is truly good, true to himself, not swayed by King, society or Church.

Despite everything, however, we suspect that Wolsey is not as bad as Cromwell. There exists between More and him a certain wary rapport and a certain respect. And in the end, it is Wolsey who names More for Chancellor, perhaps in a last attempt to right the wrong he has done and 'govern the country by prayers' (p. 12).

THE KING

It is the King, Henry VIII, who is in fact responsible for the events which form the main body of the play. An unseen hand – apart from a brief appearance in Act One (pp. 27–34) – he is nevertheless the impetus for everything that happens.

As is the case with most of the characters, Henry was a real person. The Henry we see in the play is not the old, stout person of the familiar image. He is slim, athletic, clean-shaven (Bolt specifies all this on p. xxiv), and extremely attractive in both a physical and emotional sense. Meg responds to him as a young and handsome man, More as a genuinely likeable person, who is intelligent, creative and gifted in music, dancing and athletics. Henry represents the Tudor age, the English Renaissance man, developed in mind and body, ruling a country efficiently while at the same time composing fine airs.

Conversely, of course, Henry is selfish, impetuous and used to having his own way. He is certainly prey to his appetites and subject to whims, as we see in his constant changes of mood when with Thomas. He can be angry, he can cajole and threaten. He is put out when Meg speaks better Latin than he, just as when he is thwarted in his marriage plans. And ultimately, his power and the way he uses it lead him into that corruption that only power brings.

Henry's relationship with More is always ambiguous. The King admires his Chancellor, knows his worth ('you are the man I would soonest raise' (p. 34)) and respects him. He promises when they meet that he will leave Thomas alone and not harass him about the divorce. More, in return, actually loves Henry and is loyal to him both as King and as a person whose achievements and personality he admires. More never criticizes the King, even to others. He believes Henry's actions are wrong, but still loves the person behind those actions. He is, therefore, more and more wounded by the King's treatment of him, until, when Cromwell serves the King's message that Thomas is a traitor (p. 69), he realizes that he has been betrayed.

So Henry causes More's death. He does so because he respects and admires More, and therefore cannot live with More's constant reproach on his conscience. It is impossible to say how clear Henry's conscience

is. Bolt presents him as someone who, at any rate consciously, genuinely believes that his marriage to Catherine is false and the divorce
justified. Unconsciously, however, he is not sure enough of his ground
to be unaffected by More's attitude. Deep inside, his conscience is
troubled. And he resolves this by wishing to see More proved a bad
man and his judgement wrong, so that the natural conclusion is that
More should be destroyed. But whether or not Henry's treatment of
More is consciously wrong is open to question. Bolt shows us a man
who is unable to perjure himself; someone who has too raw a conscience, rather than no conscience at all; someone who needs to convince himself of his own rightness in order to preserve himself, his
situation and his country.

For Henry is a king, responsible for a nation, and while his prime
role in the play is as an agent of More's destruction, his secondary
function is to allow us to examine the idea of kingship. Unlike today,
royal power in Tudor times was real. The monarch had absolute
control and absolute responsibility for his country. A good ruler earned
the love of the people and ensured the prosperity of the country. A bad
ruler – or uncertainty about the monarch – could destroy a nation. This
is why Wolsey is so concerned that Henry have an heir (pp. 11–12), and
why Henry is able to talk himself into divorce for the sake of his people.

Kingship is a hard and vital task: we sympathize with Henry's
problem, as More does. So More will not rebuke Henry; he supports
him, will not listen to criticism, and rebukes Norfolk for considering
breaking his 'oath of obedience' to the King (p. 53). It is imperative
for the country that, no matter what More's views, he supports Henry
as monarch.

In many ways, Henry is a good king; he leads England to prosperity,
supports learning and culture, and encourages the arts. But he also lets
his personal desires rule him. His decision to divorce Catherine may
well be so that England will have a Tudor king. Breaking from Catholicism may well be to free England from religious tyranny. But these are
not the only reasons, and Bolt presents us with ample evidence that
Henry's passions, not his kingship, made his decision. More, conversely, is sole ruler of his passions, and his ultimate obedience is not
to an earthly king, but to God and his own conscience. The message,

presented through Henry and his interaction with More, is that a country needs a good monarch, but it needs men of good conscience far more.

We learn late in the play, before More's death, that Henry's end is from syphilis. And by this time, the King is no longer a real person, just a shadowy figure to us. Nevertheless, he affects events right to the end, when More mentions him, with regret and respect, in his final speech: he is the cause and the pivot around which everything in the play has moved.

RICHARD RICH

A Man for All Seasons is centred around one man who refuses to be corrupted, to bow to society's wishes and pursue ambition and power, and so is destroyed. Parallel to the story of Thomas More, however, we are shown a man who is corrupted because he wishes to be fêted by society and gain wealth and power. He prospers, and his name is Richard Rich.

Rich's path is the total opposite of More's. We see him first, a good teacher, just beginning to study the doctrines of Machiavelli and to be influenced by Cromwell. He is by nature ambitious: he has come to London to make his way in society and is disappointed that he has not prospered.

We first see both Rich and More discussing whether a man can be bought. More claims that some men have no price, and proves this by himself resisting all attempts to buy him. Rich argues against the notion, which marks the beginning of his corruption. He moves from accepting the goblet from More, to giving Cromwell information in return for favours, and finally to perjuring himself in return for Wales. As inexorably as More moves towards death by being true to himself, Rich moves towards corruption by betraying friends, giving away secrets, and finally lying on peril of his soul and, in the view of the time, damning himself for all eternity.

Why does Rich become corrupted while More attains sainthood?

Both are intelligent; both have begun from a lowly station. Rich is not cruel, like Cromwell, nor simplistic like Norfolk. The essence of his character, however, is the total opposite of More's. Like Will Roper, with whom he may be compared, he is easily influenced, and he values external gains more than internal consistency. Society, other people's opinions, fame and respect matter to Rich. He wants to be known as a teacher, he laps up the Steward's flattery – as he does possessions too: he takes the goblet greedily to buy new clothes. So when Cromwell encourages him, praises him for giving information, and rewards him for his efforts, Rich blossoms into a man who, unlike More, is able to regard as unimportant his own damnation.

Rich's path to damnation is not a straightforward one, however. He knows what he is doing and fears it. His argument with More in Act One has all the hallmarks of a man slipping into a pattern of behaviour and defending it by claiming that everyone does it. When he returns to More's house to warn him that he is being watched, he pleads with More to employ him, and is distraught when More refuses. And all Rich's conversations with Cromwell show us his wariness as compared to Cromwell's ruthlessness. In the end, when his perjury destroys More, Rich is defensive and reluctant to face his victim. He knows what he has done.

Rich's relationship with More is a complex one. He genuinely admires Thomas, is drawn towards him not only because of Thomas's power, and genuinely desires to work for him. More in turn wants the best for the young man, but sees him clearly, and will not employ him. Rich defends Thomas to Cromwell, and almost wants More to win the battle between them: he is triumphant when Cromwell fails to frighten More. Ultimately, however, Rich's ambition triumphs over his affection, and he betrays More.

Rich's main purpose in the play is to provide a parallel and contrast with Thomas. We see Rich fail as More becomes strengthened. As Rich rises in power, More loses his Chancellorship, is jailed and condemned. Rich becomes Lord Chancellor and damned, while More is executed and canonized. One's material rise and spiritual fall is mirrored in the other's worldly downfall and sainthood.

Rich also provides a link between More and Cromwell, beginning loyal to one, ending loyal to the other; the transfer occurs in the exact centre of the play. Whereas Cromwell is seen as the epitome of evil and More as the focal point of good, Rich is a mixture, but evil triumphs in him.

Rich shows us, then, the end-product of what More prophesies will happen when a country follows a corrupt road: 'First men will disclaim their hearts and presently they will have no hearts' (p. 95).

NORFOLK

The chief source of More's pain in following his conscience during the course of the play is the non-comprehension of his family. His friend Norfolk, however, is the second point of vulnerability in his life.

Norfolk is a noble, born to riches, and used to a ruling position in society. We see, from his words and from the way others react to him, that he is not a great intellectual – and he too realizes this. He is an active man, a sportsman and a soldier; our first view of him is in an argument with Alice about falconry.

We see from the first that Norfolk is an old friend of the More family, at ease in their company, able to discuss issues, argue and joke with them, inviting Alice to ride, and employing a young man More points out to him. In Act One, there is little more we do know of Norfolk. We sense, from his reactions during the King's visit, that he is bound by convention; as a noble, he is in awe of the King, and does not understand that Thomas can regard prayers as more important than a royal visit.

It is not until Act Two, however, that we see Norfolk in more depth, when his beliefs clash with More's. Thomas is surrounded by people who for one reason or another – love, fear, ambition – want him to submit to the King's wishes. Norfolk presents another variation – a genuine belief that if everyone has submitted, then so should Thomas. This belief is founded in the fact that Norfolk is a loyal nobleman, who unquestioningly obeys the King as generations have done before him.

So Norfolk disagrees with More, refusing to help him take off the chain when he resigns the Chancellorship, and mocks him for being wary of the King's reaction. Very soon, Norfolk has to decide where his loyalties lie, for when Henry turns on More, he uses Norfolk, More's friend, as a weapon in the attack. Norfolk suffers here, for he is genuinely fond of Thomas and immovably loyal to the King. He appeals to More to change his mind; he is concerned for his friend. But More, knowing that Norfolk will pay for his friendship, deliberately breaks it off, and Norfolk is left with no option but to follow the King.

From this point on, Norfolk combines administrative action with a constant leaning towards More. We see him, in all the interrogation sessions, half siding with Thomas, unhappy at the inevitable turn of events, and yet doggedly pressing on with the course of law. By the trial (Norfolk never suspects perjury), he is entrenched in his position, and it is he who finally reads the sentence of death to his friend.

It seems in some ways that Norfolk betrays Thomas more than Cromwell or Rich do; he was his friend, yet he turned against him. But neither Cromwell nor Rich are following their consciences; they do what they do for political expediency and ambition, knowing that it is wrong. Norfolk is actually being true to himself, following his conscience – and his conscience tells him to do what everyone else does, to obey the King, to do his duty, trusting that it is for the best. This path leads him to give up More's friendship, just as it leads More to give up Norfolk's friendship.

This action of More's is very selfless, and is the beginning of the process whereby he says goodbye to all his family and friends, walking alone towards inevitable death. The way Bolt has presented More makes it imperative that he is not understood: no one really comprehends what he is doing, so that he is forced to act out of pure conscience, against society's pressure. Norfolk is part of this, pressurizing More to change his mind, then withdrawing from him. This shows us More's bravery in acting alone.

We can see, then, that Norfolk's function is to serve, as so many characters do in the play, as a representative.He represents friendship, from which Thomas must withdraw (notice the symbolic meeting and parting just before the execution). He represents the English nobility, who follow the King 'because [he] wears the crown' (p. 32). He represents those who follow their conscience by simply and blindly doing what everyone else does. He is both an influence on More and a stark contrast to him.

CHAPUYS

Thomas More acts as he does because of personal conviction that Henry should not divorce Catherine and that the Catholic Church is spiritually the true Church. Others around him pressure him to submit for varying reasons, mainly political. One person urges him to stand firm, not because he understands More's personal viewpoint, but because More's actions suit him politically. This person is Chapuys, the Spanish Ambassador. He supports More because he is using him, hoping that More's actions will prevent the divorce and serve Spanish ends. When the divorce goes through, Chapuys again tries to use More, as a figurehead for internal rebellion aimed at overthrowing the Crown and laying the way open for increased Spanish power.

Chapuys himself is not a developed character. We learn little about how he feels, reacts and thinks; he is a spokesman for Spanish–Catholic interests, somewhat of a caricature of a religious professional diplomat. He pretends to be intellectual, shrewd and political, but in fact is easily outwitted, even by More's Steward (pp. 23–4). He worships his religion unthinkingly, contrasting with Thomas's measured development of personal goodness.

We watch as Chapuys approaches More, questions his Steward, and finally, when he is sure that More is against Henry's actions, visits him. When Thomas has resigned the Chancellorship, Chapuys has the 'proof' he needs. He makes an open political overture with a letter from King Charles of Spain, and confidently expects to be greeted with open arms. Surely, if More is against the divorce and the break with Rome, he must be for Spain.

But this is not true. More is a loyal subject of England and King Henry, so he rejects Chapuys's overtures outright throughout the play. He refuses to divulge his views, refuses even to touch King Charles's letter, and informs on the Ambassador's hints of a Northern rebellion.

Chapuys, then, though not a developed character, has a vital role in the play – to show us Thomas's views even more clearly. Thomas could have been tempted to accept support from Spain, but he remains a loyal subject and resists the temptation. We learn, too, more about Thomas's character – his shrewdness in dealing with Chapuys by maintaining his silence, his realistic, down-to-earth view of religion, his political sense.

In the end then, Thomas rejects Chapuys, who rejects More in turn and fades from view, leaving More to his fate. In one ending of the play he does not appear again. In the other, we see Chapuys and Cromwell, who have throughout the play represented the opposing sides of English and Spanish interests, exiting together with the laughter of 'men who know what the world is and how to be comfortable in it' (p. 99). This perfectly symbolizes Chapuys's role in the play. He is Cromwell's opposite and equal, presenting Thomas with challenge and temptation so that we may learn and understand his character.

COMMON MAN

Perhaps the most unusual character in the play is the Common Man. He has a most important role as a linking narrator. He begins and ends the play, he introduces changes and closes scenes. He tells us when time has passed, when events have occurred and, at certain vital points in the play, shows us what has happened to various characters. The Common Man acts as a unifying feature, bringing together the differing and changing scenes and linking them.

The Common Man also, by talking directly to the audience, is able to explain and comment. He often does this ironically, with a worldly-wise humour which invites us too to judge the action in our way. In fact, the very irony often leads us to sympathize with the characters who are thus being commented on. Notice that the Common Man is the only person in the play who 'steps outside' the story to talk to us. Bolt does this deliberately, to remind us occasionally that it is a play we are watching, so that we do not get so lost in what is happening that we never stop to think about it.

However, as well as stepping outside the play, the Common Man is also involved as a character within it. Of course, he is not a single person, but an amalgamation of people who appear in a number of roles. The point Bolt is making is that we all have characteristics in common, whoever we are – Steward, Boatman, Publican, Juryman or Headsman – and the Common Man represents these characteristics. In fact, he represents us.

What is the Common Man like? He is dressed neutrally in black, so that he can don appropriate costume for each role. He is described as 'crafty, loosely benevolent' (p. xxiii). Certainly he is crafty: he tastes More's wine, tries to overcharge him for the boat-ride, manipulates Richard Rich and cleverly pretends ignorance with Cromwell in the inn. In general, he is benevolent: he is admiring of Meg, respectful of More, guilty that he cannot let More's family stay longer in the jail.

The Common Man's chief characteristic, however, is an unwillingness to be involved, to take responsibility for what is happening and to cause trouble. This is a theme which recurs constantly, as the Publican leaves Cromwell and Rich to their 'conspiracy' (p. 41), Matthew the Steward refuses to stay on in More's service when he resigns the Chancellorship, and the Boatman will not carry him home. The Jailer wishes he could let More out, but does not because he himself would suffer. In short, the Common Man's position is: 'I'm a plain simple man and just want to keep out of trouble' (p. 88).

There are, of course, two messages here. The first is that, in general, people do not interfere – and this is natural, for standing out against the crowd, getting involved and taking responsibility are dangerous, as the Common Man warns us in the alternative ending to the play. But it is also very cowardly. People did not get involved in the case of Thomas More, and so he died – and it is as much the fault of the Common Man who did not act as the fault of those like Cromwell who did. The extension of this, since the Common Man represents *us*, is that it is our fault. Of course, we were not alive when More was suffering, so we ourselves are not directly responsible for his death; but if we see a similar situation arising, and keep out of it as the Common Man did, we are responsible.

Secondly, we learn what is not clearly stated by the Common Man, that those who do make trouble, like More, are to be admired. The Common Man sees things happening that he does not believe are right – like Thomas being in jail, the verdict of guilty, the execution – and does not make a stand. People like More do; and they are the ones we should respect, emulate and follow. Thomas, not the Common Man, is the hero of the play because, though he does not survive, he has nevertheless stood up for what he believes in.

CROMWELL

Every hero needs an opponent, who stands against him and all he believes, who challenges and fights him. In *A Man for All Seasons*, More's opponent is Thomas Cromwell. Their views of life are directly opposed to each other, and when the King needs someone to challenge More, he chooses Cromwell. Cromwell opposes More, fights him with persuasion, threats and legal argument; in the end he is reduced to using perjury to condemn More and seemingly defeat him.

Who is this man who is so diametrically opposed to More? We hear of him first through the More family as a man to be frightened of, and when we meet him (p. 14) we realize why. Cromwell is 'subtle and serious' (p. xxiv), intelligent, shrewd, cunning and evil. He questions More slyly about his views and we are immediately wary of him. But, as yet, Cromwell has little power; he is still subservient to More and still respectful.

Next time we see Cromwell, however, he has gained power. He is 'the King's Ear' (p. 21), and his confidence has grown in proportion. So too has his 'outgoing will' (p. xxiv), love of power and lack of scruples. He bribes More's Steward for information and entices Rich with hints of reward. And when, at the end of Act One, Rich finally accedes, Cromwell bribes him into giving information. By this time,

Cromwell has a definite brief to make the divorce 'convenient' for the King – but as yet he sees More's opposition as minimal.

As More's opposition becomes more clear, however, so does Cromwell's lack of scruples. He attempts to pressure More with a charge of bribery and, when this fails, he calls him to answer charges of colluding in treason with the 'Holy Maid of Kent', and of writing a pro-Catholic book. All these strategies fail, and now Cromwell's true colours show. He has previously contented himself with trying to catch More out; now he starts perverting the course of justice. He first creates a law, complete with oath, which traps More into either giving his consent to Henry's actions or going to jail. More goes to jail – and his stubborn silence impedes Cromwell.

Finally, totally frustrated, Cromwell abandons all moral and legal principles and arranges false evidence to trap More. This is his lowest act, for which he is actually more culpable than the biddable Rich – for Cromwell feels no remorse for what he does in executing a man for the sake of 'convenience'.

Why does Cromwell act as he does? His first motivation is a simple love of power. During the course of the play he rises step by step to greater and greater heights (he eventually becomes Chancellor himself), and loves it. He also revels in those touches of personal power which mark him as truly evil: putting Rich down, playing him like a fish, controlling and corrupting him by approval and favours; manipulating Norfolk with threats of the King's displeasure; treating the woman, the Publican and the Steward with barely disguised contempt. We even get the impression that Cromwell manipulates the King in many ways.

We must remember, though, that Cromwell's other motivation for his actions is political and personal expediency. The King is pressuring him to make More submit; this must be done in order for the monarch to be content and the country to be stable. In addition, he actually does believe that it is better to bribe, lie, pervert justice and kill in order to make things 'convenient'. He always justifies his deeds in the name of 'effective action' (p. xxiv). By the end of the play, we suspect that he has forfeited all his conscience for the sake of advancement, while More has forfeited his advancement in order to follow his conscience.

The two hate each other; More hates Cromwell's pragmatism, lack of conscience, cruelty and ambition. Cromwell despises what he sees as More's self-indulgent goodness, lack of political expediency and cowardice in not speaking out. In the final trial, they face each other, these opposites of good and evil – as antagonists, hero and villain.

And, so it seems, Cromwell wins. More is condemned and executed, and Cromwell and Chapuys exit as men who 'know how to be comfortable' in the world (p. 99). In fact, however, it is More who ultimately triumphs, for in his terms, he will go to God contented, having lived a life true to himself; Cromwell too is eventually executed for treason and, by contrast, will die knowing he has given up everything to gain worldly power.

THOMAS MORE

Thomas More is the central character in the play, and the 'man for all seasons' of the title. He was also a real, historical person. Bolt says in his preface that he chose More as a hero because he was attracted to his 'sense of his own self' (p. xii) and his 'splendid social adjustment' (p. xv).

What was Thomas's own self? As presented in the play – and Bolt keeps very close to the historical accounts, even using Thomas's own words at many points – he is a true Renaissance man. He is highly intelligent, proud of that bright mind which allows him to serve God, and he delights in those leaps of logic which annoy Norfolk. He is also highly educated, and has his children well educated too. He makes sure he is up to date with contemporary writing, such as Machiavelli's. And we know from historical accounts (as Bolt is aware) that Thomas 'corresponded with the greatest minds in Europe as the ... acknowledged champion of the new Learning in England' (p. xiv).

More began his career as a lawyer, and must have been a highly successful one. He soon rose in fame and station to be a knight, and entered the world of politics as an ambassador. We know the King both respected him professionally and admired him personally, and his appointment as Lord Chancellor was both expected and welcomed. He was, quite simply, good at his work, and we see evidence of this in his handling of the law, which is both expert and intuitive, based on a real belief that the legal system works and is valid, and in his dealings with those such as Cromwell and Chapuys, which show a skilful use of craft and diplomacy.

Not only is More's mental life varied, but he is capable of another side, his emotional life. He is able, we hear, to show 'mirth and gravity': he can be emotionally flexible. He is seen discussing his beliefs with great seriousness. He feels affection and warmth for his family and friends. Conversely, we see him angry with Norfolk and Roper – to whom he almost immediately apologizes sincerely. We see Thomas making jokes, even when we might think life is at its lowest ebb. He can bear the rigours of jail with a smile, though the depth of his despair is also obvious when he bids goodbye to Alice.

What else constitutes Thomas's self, if not his mental and emotional life? His spirituality is, in fact, more vital to him than both of these. He firmly believes in God, and that the expression of God on earth is to be found in the Catholic Church. It is, of course, irrelevant whether we agree with this; 'I believe it,' says More (p. 53), and this is what is important. More's religious life is an integral part of himself: he naturally says bedtime prayers; he goes to vespers even when the King is due to visit. He has a real and lively sense of God and of the ways he can serve him. He truly believes that the Catholic Church is the correct one, and that in matters of morals it speaks with God's voice.

These, then, are the pillars of More's self – his mental brightness, his emotional flexibility and his religious belief. How does this self relate to people, showing the 'splendid social adjustment' Bolt admires?

The answer is: very well. More is first and foremost a family man; his family adore him. He loves his wife, though their relationship is stormy; we see this from the quiet way he tries to please Alice and make her happy, and from the heart-rending scene in the jail when he shows that he needs her love in order to carry through his beliefs: 'If you say that, Alice, I don't see how I'm to face it' (p. 86).

To his daughter, More is consistently kind, gentle and under- standing; he is proud of her intelligence, which he has developed, and

glad to see her happy with Roper. At only two points does he stick —
when Meg tries to persuade him to renege, and in refusing the marriage
between Meg and Roper when Roper is a heretic. The first comes from
the vulnerability of a man who is disappointed that someone he loves
does not trust him to do what he thinks is right. The second is a loving
act of duty by a father who genuinely believes it dangerous for his
daughter to marry out of the Church.

For More, though he is fond of Roper and gets on well with him,
mistrusts his principles. He almost enjoys arguing with Will, certainly
likes teasing him, and is at ease with him socially. It is only when
worried by Roper's inconsistency that More draws back and is concerned.

Outside the family, More is also liked. He obviously has a deep and
warm relationship with Norfolk, which has stood the test of time. They
respect each other, and Norfolk is genuinely grieved at More's actions:
'You'll break my heart' (p. 71). It says much for Thomas's selflessness
that he deliberately destroys this friendship in order to protect Norfolk.

Politically, as we have seen, More is successful. He is respected by
Wolsey, who names him for Chancellor. He is known as a powerful man
by both Cromwell and Chapuys, and until the final betrayal, he
skilfully plays them off against each other. And More is also loyal to
the King.

Thomas's relationship with Henry is a strange combination: he
admires and is loyal to the King, both for the country's sake and
because he personally likes him. Henry returns the admiration — but
it is just this emotional dependence on Thomas that makes the King
need Thomas's approval and, when he does not get it, strike out.

The final group of people More relates to are those socially beneath
him. He treats servants and those dependent on him with consistent
care and justice; he gives the correct verdict on Catherine Anger's
lawsuit , and expects Matthew to inform on him. More's dealings with
Rich are a perfect mark of his goodness: he combines understanding
with good advice, without being manipulated by Rich, and finally
forgives him.

What we see, then, is an intelligent, educated, kind and human man,
who has a full range of relationships with all sorts of people and is

'almost indecently' successful (p. xiv). Why, then, does he find it necessary to give up the life that contains all this, because of what he believes?

The answer seems to be, as expressed in the play, that More's self was inextricably bound up with his beliefs, and that when the society to which he 'adjusted' demanded he deny these beliefs, he had to say no.

There are numerous instances in the play when More explains that in taking an oath to what he does not believe, he is denying his very self: for instance, '[I] needn't hope to find [myself] again' (p. 83). It is unfortunate that society is twisted enough to put him to death because of this, but it does not alter the facts for More. He truly believes that by taking the oath he is betraying the 'little area ... where I must rule myself' (p. 35), and that perjuring himself would result in a life spent in hell. The ultimate conclusion is inescapable, and Thomas goes to his death. When given the choice between self and society, he chose self, and an eternal heaven. You will find a detailed discussion of the issues raised by More's martyrdom on pp. 87–91.

Commentary

HISTORICAL BACKGROUND

A Man for All Seasons is a play based on actual historical events. In order to understand the play, therefore, we need to understand the background to the events it covers.

Tudor England was a country just recovering from a series of civil wars between the rival families of York and Lancaster. The previous Yorkist King, Richard III, had been defeated and killed; the Lancastrian who took the throne after him in 1485 was the Tudor Henry VII. He set England on an affluent and peaceful course, strengthening her, and encouraging alliances with other European powers; the Tudor era was seen at the time, as it still is, as an optimistic age for the English people.

Henry VII's eldest son, Arthur, who was heir to the throne, made an advantageous marriage with a Spanish princess, Catherine of Aragon. This alliance was welcomed by both England and Spain as a road to political peace, ensuring that neither country would attack the other. When Arthur died before succeeding to the throne, both sides were eager for Catherine to remain linked to the English royal family. A perfect solution seemed to be for her to marry Arthur's younger brother, Henry.

However, there was one barrier to this – such a marriage was forbidden by the Catholic Church. At the time, all the known Western world held one unified religion, Catholicism. Its head was the Pope, whose power over all the people of Christendom was believed to come directly from God. Certainly the Church had achieved much good, providing a comforting belief for many and a stable social structure within which society operated, and encouraging education, good works and spiritual growth. However, many of the highest men in the Church – as in all positions of power at that time – were corrupt, and charged for their spiritual services, indulged their vices and totally contradicted the virtues they preached.

Both the English and Spanish royal families were, however, devout Catholics. They submitted to the Pope their request that Henry and Catherine be allowed to marry. After consideration, a dispensation was granted, and the couple were wed. For a long while, the marriage worked. Henry became King on his father's death, and Catherine was his Queen. England continued to flourish under Tudor rule.

Throughout Europe, meanwhile, criticism of the Catholic Church was mounting. In Germany, Martin Luther spoke out against corruption, and about some of the basic beliefs of Catholicism, such as the Seven Sacraments. In reply, many of the staunch Catholic countries, such as Spain and England, supported the Church. Henry VIII himself wrote *A Defence of the Seven Sacraments* in 1521, for which he received the gratitude of the Pope in the form of an honourable title, Fidei Defensor, Defender of the Faith (the rulers of England retain this title to the present day, and if you look on the back of English coins, you will find inscribed around the sovereign's head the initial letters of those words).

But times and minds change. Within a few years, Henry's commitment both to his Queen and to his Church had begun to waver. The reasons seem to be these. Firstly, Catherine, who was older than Henry, grew unattractive and undesirable. She turned more and more to the comfort of religion, and the relationship between husband and wife began to fail. In addition, Henry, whose sexual appetites had always strayed beyond the marriage bed, had found a new young love, Anne Boleyn. Anne, whose sister had already been Henry's mistress, may have been in love, or may have cold-bloodedly planned to become Queen. Whatever *her* motives, Henry's soon hardened into a conscious desire to marry her.

His wish was also founded on what seemed to many at the time to be sound political sense. There had never been a Queen of England – anything other than a King was unthinkable. So when Henry died, there needed to be a male heir to succeed him. And of Catherine's many children, only a girl – Mary – had survived. Henry and his ministers, the memory of recent civil wars too clearly with them, foresaw more wranglings for succession if there was no son, and feared the disastrous effect on England. What followed was, therefore, in part motivated by a desire to avoid this. (It is ironic that in fact Catherine's daughter did gain the throne and was succeeded by another Queen, her half-sister Elizabeth, who ruled for a glorious forty-five years, which were the high point of the Tudor dynasty.)

The issue of whether Henry should have ever married Catherine was, the King now began to think, in question. Surely a marriage that had gone so disastrously wrong, and had resulted only in one daughter, could not be blessed by God? Henry convinced himself that he must, in fact, be living in a state of sin, and had been since he married Catherine. The sooner he was free, the better.

For these, and possibly many other reasons, Henry decided that his best course of action was to put away Catherine and marry Anne, and it is at this point that *A Man for All Seasons* opens. The King's first step was to approach the head of the Catholic Church and ask for a reversal of the original dispensation which allowed him to marry Catherine; this would annul their marriage. Henry instructed his Lord Chancellor, the shrewd but corrupt Cardinal Wolsey, to write to the Pope, and hint at rebellion against the Church if the request was not met. It is this letter which Wolsey has prepared in Act One, and which he shows to More (p. 10), discussing the reasons for it as he does so. More is at the time uneasy about the reasons for Henry's plea to the Church, but has no direct part in what is happening.

The response from Rome was direct and negative. For many reasons, the Church rejected Henry's request and decreed that the marriage with Catherine should stand. The Pope at the time must have been much influenced by the Spaniards, who had recently attacked and sacked Rome; obviously they did not wish their Princess Catherine to be unceremoniously put away by her foreign husband. In addition, the Pope may well have had sound theological reasons for not wishing to reverse his decision – or he may simply have objected to Henry's wish for 'marriage on demand'.

Henry was now left with a seemingly impossible situation. To divorce Catherine and marry Anne would be to call down excommunication (expulsion) from the Catholic Church which did not accept divorce as moral. In a Catholic country, this would have made his position as ruler very vulnerable. The alternative – to stay with Catherine – seemed unthinkable from both the personal and political aspects. Henry's first reaction, as we learn on p. 20 of the play, was to remove from office the man who had failed to convince the Pope to agree: Cardinal Wolsey was removed from his Lord Chancellorship (and later accused of treason and died). In his place Sir Thomas More was elected.

It is in this position that we find More in the later part of Act One. He was always concerned lest he should become involved in a situation which would obviously challenge his loyalty to both Church and King. However, Henry assured Thomas that he would not be challenged on the divorce question (during his visit to Chelsea, pp. 30–34). He accepted the position of Lord Chancellor, and served excellently and honestly.

In the meantime, however, Henry was becoming more determined to marry Anne, and more convinced that the Pope was wrong in his decision. Remember that his increasing disillusionment with the Catholic Church was set against a general discontent throughout Europe; many countries formed their own independent churches at that time.

So Henry came to the point at which we see him in Act One. What his ultimate motives were is a point of contention; it is likely that he wanted the Pope overruled and honestly believed that the decision was incorrect. It is possible that he saw the Church as corrupt and felt that he could create an uncorrupted Church. It is likely that he simply wanted his own way. Whatever the reasons, in 1531 Henry found his way: he presented the country with an Act of Parliament which stated that he, not the Pope, was head of the Church in his country, thus establishing the Church of England as a separate entity, the point in the play at which Act Two opens. The nobles and the Commons agreed; More, however, was unhappy. When the Church leaders of England and Scotland gave tacit consent, he found himself unable to do so, and resigned his Chancellorship, as we see on p. 52. He believed that, however corrupt the Church, the Pope was divinely guided to lead it, and that Henry could not usurp this place and set up his own Church in England.

Although the King promised not to involve Thomas in the matter, More's status in the country was such that his resignation seemed a criticism of Henry's action. Henry needed Thomas's support, probably on a personal level – for he valued his very real friendship and, it is hinted, did not feel at ease with his conscience – but certainly on a political level, to give credibility to his actions. Henry was already wary of Thomas's effect; from the resignation onward, however, More was probably a marked man. Henry became more and more convinced of his 'treachery'. Cromwell a politician whose rise to Lord Chancellor we see during the play, was given the task of challenging More and trying to persuade him to support the Act of Supremacy; Cromwell used accusations of bribery (p. 58ff.) and of treachery (p. 67ff.), and threats (p. 69). To every attempt, More shrewdly remained silent, knowing that in law no action could be taken against him without evidence. He also avoided the temptation to side with Spain or support anti-royalist feeling in England (p. 63).

Having established a separate Church in England, Henry had power over its officers. Cranmer, appointed Archbishop of Canterbury, was easily persuaded to grant Henry the divorce from Catherine, and soon after, the King married Anne Boleyn. At all this, Thomas remained silent, but we know that he disagreed with the King's actions.

In order to protect Queen Anne's hoped-for sons, Henry then proposed an Act of Succession, proclaiming his heirs by Anne legitimate. He badly needed public approval of this Act by figures of State in order to offset real resistance to his actions. Many of the common people, particularly in Scotland and the North, were rebelling against his dissolution of their beloved religion and the ensuing attacks on the churches and monasteries. In addition, Spain was outraged at his treatment of Queen Catherine.

To gain the support he needed, Henry insisted that all should take an oath upholding the Act of Succession (p. 74). Thomas, who disagreed both with the divorce and the break with the Catholic Church, was in a quandary. He could keep silent; but to him, an oath was a real statement before a real God, and if he took the oath, he would be damned for ever, a far more frightening fate to him than death.

However, Henry's personal and political ends were not satisfied with Thomas's silence: they needed his public oath. Thomas was imprisoned (p. 75) and questioned (p. 76ff.); he kept his silence, and would neither take the oath nor say why. For not taking the oath, as he explains on p. 78, his goods were forfeit and he was imprisoned; but had he spoken out against the King's actions, he would be executed as a traitor. Finally, Cromwell lost patience. He rigged evidence that More had denied the Act of Supremacy, and so had effectively denied that the King was head of the Church, a treasonable act (pp. 93–4). More was brought to trial (p. 88ff.) and found guilty (p. 97).

At this point, More was finally free to speak out. The play here uses many of his actual words, taken from the trial. He stated what many had suspected – though they previously had no proof – that he did consider the breach with the Catholic Church wrong and Henry's claim to be head of the Church of England false (pp. 96–7). But as More pointed out, it was his opposition to the divorce and marriage which had led to his death, by denying Henry the personal approval he needed for his acts.

More was executed (p. 99). The ends of all the other characters, as we are told in the play (p. 75) varied: Norfolk narrowly escaped execution, Cromwell was executed, Rich prospered. King Henry's marriage to Queen Anne bore only dead sons, and he finally had his wife beheaded for treason. The King married four times more, gained the son he wanted, and eventually died of syphilis. The Tudor dynasty continued, despite Henry's fears, with two Queens among it.

Thomas More was created a saint by the Catholic Church, which never regained its influence in England. More is, however, recognized as a great and good man by people of all religions, because he followed his conscience.

A MAN FOR ALL SEASONS

Robert Bolt called his play *A Man for All Seasons*. The man referred to is, of course, Thomas More, the hero of the play, a sixteenth-century statesman and martyr. But what does Bolt mean by 'all seasons'? And why does he choose a Tudor martyr as the focal point for a twentieth-century drama?

Perhaps our starting-point could be the quotations with which Bolt prefaces the play. One of them, by Robert Whittinton, contains the epithet 'a man for all seasons'. By it, Whittinton firstly means More's variety in characteristics and in behaviour: 'as time requireth', he is a man of 'mirth' and of 'gravity'. More can adapt to situations flexibly. But there is surely also a further, more vital meaning to be taken from the phrase. For if the word 'seasons' is read to mean 'times' or 'ages', then Thomas is undoubtedly a man whose beliefs and actions are relevant to all ages. This answers the query concerning Bolt's choice of hero; for whether a man is born in the sixteenth century or the twentieth, if he has attributes from which we may learn and which we may admire, then it is still relevant today to write a play about him.

Let us look first, then, at More's flexibility. He is indeed a man capable of handling all situations. He is a family man, able to make his relationship with a none-too-placid wife work well, yet maintain his household control. He relates equally well to uneducated Alice and highly educated Margaret. He can be both fond of Roper and intransigent in stopping his marriage to Meg when it is unwise. Politically, More is diplomatic; he will not bend to Wolsey or to the King, but he combines this with tact and wit, which make him successful and popular. He can be unmoving when tempted by Chapuys to disloyalty, and yet increasingly soft-hearted with his servants.

We see too that More has a wide range of emotions; he is not a serious intellectual pedant, but a man whose fierce intelligence is offset by genuine vulnerability and a bright sense of humour. Minutes after raging at Roper about his morals, he is apologizing and joking with him. He can be in the depths of despair in jail, yet still think of sharing his precious food with Bishop Fisher. And at the climax of the play, he combines genuine fear, genuine courage and real forgiveness for Rich's betrayal.

More's flexibility, then, makes him a 'man for all seasons' in one sense of the phrase. In the other sense, it is his inflexibility which make him so. For it is More's ability to stand against fear and suffering, society's pressure, and personal temptation, and be true to himself and his conscience which makes his story relevant to us.

More's progress towards the ultimate conclusion of the play shows clearly all these points. Here is a man who is successful, loved, respected – and who enjoys his life in a worldly as well as a spiritual sense. When Henry asks for his approval of the divorce and the subsequent break from the Catholic Church, he cannot give this. He tells the King this clearly, but also does not speak out publicly against the affair. He keeps silent, and continues to do so until faced by a society which demands that he swear an oath to God that he believes what he does not believe. This More cannot do, because for him, as he clearly states thoroughout the play, this would be denying himself, and would mean, for him, hell for all eternity, and separation fom his God.

It is possibly difficult for us today to understand More's position – that he was prepared to die rather than lie to God about what he believed. Certainly in his own time, few people really understood More's position, as we see in the play. But for Thomas, being the person he was, if society offered him a choice between death and denying his true self, the choice was easy.

There are many factors about this choice, and the man who made it, which Bolt presents for our examination and ultimate admiration. Perhaps the first is that More does not go to his death unknowingly. We see right from the start, in his conversation with Wolsey, that More knows what may happen, and is genuinely afraid. This fear builds with each new event – the approaches by Chapuys and Cromwell, the resignation, the questioning – and while More strives harder to keep his family unafraid, he himself becomes more so. He watches the poverty affect not only his family's way of life but also their attitude towards him. He goes to jail afraid, suffers there, and is in real anguish at the thought of 'the worst that they may do to me' (p. 85). Nevertheless, despite his awareness of what is happening, despite his real fear, despite the pain that he endures through his own suffering and that of his family, More still does not waver; he fights that part of him which must have been eager to give in, and stands firm.

Pressure on More does not only come from within him, however: there is a great deal of pressure from outside. More is acting against the whole weight of the King's power, which is shown by Wolsey, Cromwell, Cranmer and the King himself. He has to stand out against persuasion, cajolery, and then threats, argument and force. Perhaps the hardest for More to resist are the King's own pleas, during his visit, for More admires Henry greatly; but in the end, 'I can *not* come with Your Grace' (p. 31). Neither is all the pressure from above. Norfolk, More's friend, begs him to submit. Alice spends most of the course of the play berating him for his actions, and even Meg tries to persuade him to change his mind during their conversation in jail.

To all these pressures, More is vulnerable but unwavered. Only with Alice does he seem near to breaking, until her love supports him. This unwavered vulnerability is one of the factors which make More so attractive to us.

While resisting pressure, More equally cannot be bought. It is significant that the first time we see him, More is deep in conversation with Rich on whether 'every man has his price' (p. 2). Rich says yes – and he is bought by Wales. More denies it – and he proves his belief by himself being unpurchasable. The King offers More favours and lands, both before his resignation and, by implication, even afterwards; but the same spirit which prevents More from accepting Catherine Anger's bribe leads him to refuse Henry's offers.

The only interest More shows, in this first conversation with Rich, is in the idea of a man's being bought 'with suffering' (p. 2) – the appeal, to some men, of martyrdom. To a world with a Catholic viewpoint, martyrdom had advantages – an assured place in heaven for all eternity, and sainthood within the Church. Certainly More may have been tempted by the prospect of martyrdom, but he also seems to have been very aware of this temptation, and the lengths he takes to avoid it also make us admire him. He never courts danger, is intractably silent in order to protect himself and his family, and fights with all the legal and intellectual means at his disposal to evade death. When it comes, it is through perjury: More does not seek it.

What we have, then, is a man who tries to avoid martyrdom, but ultimately chooses it rather than betray himself. It may seem, from Thomas's point of view, as if he had no choice: 'I was not able to continue. I would have if I could!' (p. 55). But Bolt also presents us, to show the value of More's actions, with a number of possible alternatives More could have taken – and others in the play do. Cromwell, for example, faces the whole divorce issue as an issue of 'convenience'. For him, as for Wolsey, conscience is 'a miserable thing' (p. 93), and should be disregarded for convenience's sake. Rich too follows this doctrine, though uncertain to the end, but whereas we guess that Cromwell has placed worldly convenience first for a long time, we actually see Rich choosing to betray himself, to swear (before God) to what he knows is not true in exchange for convenience and personal worldly gain.

In various measures, too, all the other characters place conscience second to the attractions of worldly life, choosing the here and now rather than the ultimate gain of heaven and a sense of selfhood. Norfolk chooses duty as his way out and urges that More submit 'for fellowship' (p. 78). Roper's ideals change like the wind 'if the weather turns nasty' (p. 41): he has no real self to cling to. Alice sees the normal pleasures of family life as more important than More's beliefs. Even Meg, in the last analysis, does not want her father to die, and urges him to choose survival at the price of conscience. The Common Man, using the lowest common denominator of advice, simply ends the play with 'don't make trouble' (p. 100).

In contrast, More himself is, as Rich describes him, 'innocent' (p. 44). He simply and straightforwardly puts God first and the world second, even though he loves the world of wine, custards and grandchildren that he is leaving. It is Thomas who is in church when the King arrives, and is shocked at any alternative suggestion; Thomas whose God is love, and who 'must rule [him]self' (p. 35); Thomas who, once sentence has been passed, is at peace with himself and 'blithe'

(p. 99) to go to God. More is indeed innocent and unworldly, and, alone among all the other characters in the play, puts his conscience firmly first. At any time during the course of events, he could have said 'Stop', and have saved himself by a word. He does not.

The fact that More is the only character who does this is not just a dramatic device. It is a warning of what may happen if we do not follow his example. For 'first men will disclaim their hearts and presently they will have no hearts' (p. 95). More warns Cromwell, and us, that the world has few enough people who will follow their true selves, and that the implications of this are serious for mankind. Maybe we need martyrs such as More to contradict the fact that vices 'commonly profit far beyond' (p. 84) virtues. You might like to think of those contemporary martyrs who have been willing to give up everything for their beliefs, and judge what they contribute to our world today.

In the end, then, More is the centre of the play. The plot shows us how he goes to his death; the other characters are all present to lead him there. And it is his death, the choice he takes, that makes Thomas More a man for all seasons, including our own.

THE LAW

What do we mean by the law? In *A Man for All Seasons*, the law is spoken of constantly, as Thomas moves through the legal process to his death. He has a clear and proud ideal of the law, what it is and how it should be used to protect society. It is ironic, then, that it is through misuse of the law that he is eventually betrayed and condemned.

Through More, Robert Bolt defines the law as far more than a set of regulations. Whereas More sees morality as a personal system of good and evil developed from man's relationship with God, he views the law as a social system of guidelines developed from society's needs. Thomas distinguishes clearly between the two in his conversation with Roper (p. 38), where he refuses to allow Will to arrest Rich because, though he may be a morally bad man, he has not transgressed any law. Sin is punished by God; man may only punish those who break society's rules through the legal system.

How does More view society's rules, then? He is himself a lawyer, a good one, and proud of it. His intelligence and talent in the field have raised him high. And he glories in his talent – 'I doubt if there's a man alive who could follow me there' (p. 39) – loving to argue, using logic step by step to prove or disprove a theory. Norfolk calls them 'lawyer's tricks' (p. 53), but they are sound logical arguments, upon which the law is based.

More glories not only in his grasp of the law, but in the law itself. He sees it, firstly, as a protection for those who are victims of crime, used to prosecute the guilty. He sees it also as a protection for the innocent; properly used, the law will give a correct judgement, acquitting the innocent even if charged. So More gives the correct judgement in the Court of Requests, even though Catherine Anger complains, protecting the innocent, punishing the guilty.

It is because of More's confidence in the law that he relies on it throughout the play. When the storm clouds begin to gather, and Henry's forces begin to close in, Thomas is confident, because he has done no wrong, and knows full well how to protect himself legally. He does not trust the people around him, who, he knows, have their weaknesses and corruptions, but he trusts the knots and tangles of the law on which he has always relied. 'Justice is what you're threatened with,' declares Cromwell, and More replies happily, 'Then I'm not threatened' (p. 79).

And indeed, until the final trial, More is protected by justice. The trumped-up bribery charge over the case of Catherine Anger is dropped. By protecting himself with witnesses and witnessed letters, More escapes the charge of treason in the matter of the 'Holy Maid of Kent'. And when the issue of who wrote the book *A Defence of the Seven Sacraments* is raised, More is able to disarm the opposition by pointing out that the case would require the King to swear a falsehood, which he will not do.

More's greatest safety net, however, in the legal sense, is his silence. He knows that by law, unless he clearly states treasonable grounds for his actions, he cannot be convicted of treason. So he keeps quiet, despite pressure from his family, and although imprisoned for not taking the oath on the Act of Succession, he is legally safe from further harm.

Unhappily, however, not everyone in society has the same view as More of society's laws. To some, like Alice and Norfolk, they are irritations which they do not quite comprehend. Norfolk needs a careful explanation by More of the legal points concerned before he is really able to understand what is going on (p. 78) – and thereafter is totally gulled by the proceedings, including Rich's perjury. Alice is only concerned with More's silence, which seems to her a lack of trust, until he explains the legal implications of her knowing anything at all about his views (p. 56).

To some people, the law is a hindrance which must be done away with. Strangely, the two people who agree on this, did they but know it, are two otherwise totally opposed characters, Roper and Cromwell. Roper, in the cause of religion, would do away with the laws. He feels they protect not only the innocent, but also the guilty, and he points to Richard Rich as an example of an evil man who has escaped punishment because the law defends him. When More argues, Roper accuses him of worshipping the law, preferring it to God, morality and religion. More's answer to this is to remind Roper that Man is not God. God judges between right and wrong; Man can only wield the law in the best way he knows how.

Roper at least bases his criticism of the law on a desire to rid the country of evil. Cromwell, on the other hand, has no justification for his manipulation of the law other than the criterion of 'convenience' (p. 44). In order to make Henry's divorce easy, and neutralize the inconvenience of Sir Thomas More, Cromwell first attempts to accuse him wrongly of bribery, then of treason on two separate cases (pp. 68–9). On both occasions he is blocked from pressing these charges by More's legal skill; and it is with real hatred that Cromwell then decides to pervert the course of justice even further.

For it is not to bring good to society, or to prevent evil, that Cromwell brings the new Act through Parliament, legally demanding an oath: 'It's just a matter of finding the right law. Or making one' (p. 61). It is solely to make More submit, to ease Henry's conscience, to make things more convenient. Cromwell twists the laws to his own specifications, and in so doing totally negates their power.

We see, then, More, with his rock-steady belief in and dependence on the law, facing an opponent who regards the law as second to 'convenience'. What More does not realize, in his innocence, is that the law, made by imperfect man, can just as easily be perverted by that same imperfect man. His sense of security is wrongly founded.

So we come to the high point of the workings of justice – Thomas's trial. Bolt precedes it with an ironic hymn of praise to the Law:

> *What Englishman can behold without Awe*
> *The Canvas and the Rigging of the Law!*

The scenery reflects this sense of occasion.

The Council members preside, and there is also a jury, as there must always be in British law, of twelve men. The Common Man unwillingly takes the role of Foreman. We thus have the full panoply of justice, which is about to be misused.

The misuse occurs in several ways. Firstly, the whole basis of the charge is false: as Thomas points out (p. 90), he cannot be accused of treason for refusing to take the oath, only for refusing it because he denies Henry's title. More's objections are overruled, in a welter of bullying threats which are also contrary to the objective mode the law should use, and the trial continues.

Next, Cromwell argues, illogically, that Thomas's silence means he does not agree with what is happening. Thomas points out that in law the opposite is true: 'Silence Gives Consent.' It may be, as Cromwell suggests, that the world considers Thomas's silence to mean lack of consent, but in a court of law, the world's views are not important: 'This Court must construe according to the law' (p. 92).

Then Richard Rich appears. He gives evidence that More denied the King's title, thus perjuring himself and not only damning his soul, but perverting the cause of justice. The fact that this happens not only betrays More and literally causes his death. It also shows him – and us – that the legal system is vulnerable. Man-made laws, set up to protect society, can themselves be twisted by men, whose ambition and greed come before their wish to do good, and therefore harm society.

More does, first, attempt to argue within the legal system to save himself: Rich stands firm on his testimony and, it is clear, the other two witnesses have been bought off. More realizes he can go no further: 'I am a dead man' (p. 95). A jury gives the verdict, obviously under pressure from Cromwell, another perversion of justice. He prepares to give his final speech and then go to his death.

That More is condemned and executed, despite the fact that he has broken no law, is very significant. More has always believed, and acted on the belief, that the law deals not with the workings of men's consciences, but with their actions. In the final analysis, this belief is challenged. More is punished under the law, not for what he has done, but for his conscience — 'the thoughts of my heart' (p. 95). This is a gross misuse of the law and, as More points out, lays the way open for an evil society, where people are afraid to follow their consciences, and will therefore soon have no consciences.

Ultimately, then, society's laws fail More. He has believed he is safe, and relied on that belief; and he is betrayed. Society will not accept the way he follows his sense of selfhood, has rejected him, and has misused its laws to punish him for it. It is, then, with some sense of relief, perhaps, that More withdraws from society, glad not to be part of it; his belief in the law has let him down, but his belief in God does not, and he happily turns to God in his final moments.

RELIGIOUS BELIEFS

Nowadays, a person may well be morally and ethically good, yet still not follow a religion. In order to appreciate *A Man for All Seasons* fully, it is important to understand that in Tudor times religion and morality were closely interlinked. To be a good person and yet not follow a religion was difficult, and for many, following the wrong religion meant a person was on the way to damnation.

The Catholic Church had developed from the teachings of Christ one and a half thousand years before. The Eastern sector of the Church had split away, but the Western form had spread throughout the known

Western world and was a unified religion: everyone adhered to it, and accepted the overall rule of the Pope as its head. The Church served many good purposes, providing a social framework within which people could operate, a community support system for the old and the needy, and an ethical viewpoint which stressed love and charity to others. In many ways, of course, the Church failed. The man-made institution that was the Church had contradicted and twisted many of Christ's original ideas, and the rigid hierarchy within it had encouraged those with power to become corrupt and greedy, charging for their spiritual services and ignoring the Church's rules.

At the time the play opens, revolt was just beginning. Criticism had come from many sources, chief among them Martin Luther in Germany; in reply to this, Henry wrote *A Defence of the Seven Sacraments*. In addition, physical attack on the Pope in Rome was being carried out by Spanish troops. The Catholic Church was very vulnerable and in fact, as we see, factions in several European countries broke away during the sixteenth century and formed their own reformed churches.

We have seen in other sections of this book how the characters in the play integrated basic ideas of morality, conscience, good and evil into their lives. Their reactions vary from a balanced, committed love of God and dedication to conscience, to a complete disregard for moral values as second to the cause of 'convenience'. However, people's view of the religion of the time also vary – and sometimes are at odds with their morality and goodness. Reactions to the break from Catholicism in England also varied: for some, it was a scarcely noticeable political change; for Thomas, it began a course of events leading to his death.

There are people in the play, as in real life, for whom the form of religion is not an important part of their lives, though they see God as a real person on whom they depend. Alice is one of these: she is a good-hearted woman, who naturally and 'as a matter of routine' (p. 8) says her prayers, calls on God to help her, and believes in the Catholic religion. But unlike More, Alice sees no real problem when Henry goes through with the divorce against the wishes of the head of the Church, and then breaks with Rome. She cannot understand why Thomas cannot submit, for it is not a vital matter to her. Even at the end, the religious question is not clear to her; her way of dealing with the situation is to turn back to God, who is very real to her, and trust him: 'if you go – well God knows why, I suppose' (p. 86).

Norfolk holds his religion in the same way as Alice; an area which his conscience is quite happy to relegate to second place. He, however, does not even have Alice's practical sense of God as real. His moral code and his attitude to the Church are both subservient to what Bolt calls his 'rigid adherence to the minimal code of conventional duty' (p. xxiii). A kind man and a good friend, he nevertheless is quite happy to follow the King's lead in splitting from Rome, simply because it is his duty. As for any real sense of God and spirituality, as More says, Norfolk's kind 'would have snored through the Sermon on the Mount' (p. 72).

Roper, however, is a different case. He too is a good man, for whom religion is 'his cross, his solace, and his hobby' (p. xxiv). He is compulsive about the outward signs of religion, the rules and tenets; yet he has no clear principles, and changes them easily. As a result, he changes his religion too. We see him, early in the play, a Lutheran, disgusted by the excesses of the Catholic Church. A little later he has altered, supporting the Church and its doctrines fervently. He is easily influenced, and this is his main failing, for otherwise he is kind, considerate and, later in the play, a genuine support to More – but Roper warns us what can happen when we become absorbed in the outward signs of religion without integrating the accompanying morality into our lives.

The outward signs of religion are very apparent in the lives of the two clergymen in the play and the religious Chapuys. All three have power because of religion. Wolsey, the Cardinal, misuses his place to get all the worldly power he needs; has no real sense of integrated religion and mocks More for wanting to rule the country with prayers. Chapuys makes a great show of defending the Catholic religion of Spain and is forcibly brought down to earth by More on occasion for confusing real morality with the forms of religion such as the Latin language. Cranmer, though an Archbishop, seems to have little interest in spirituality; he sees his post as a 'job of administration' (p. xxiv) – but we sense envy of Thomas for his holiness, and we know that Cranmer himself died a martyr a few years after More.

Chapuys and Cranmer represent opposite sides once the split with Rome has occurred. Both take their places for purely political reasons. Chapuys, the Spanish Ambassador, naturally upholds the Catholic religion of his country. Cranmer, we get the impression, has been made Archbishop by Henry because he is biddable, and keeps the post for political expediency. It is worth comparing with both positions Thomas's reaction to the split, which is based on deep personal soul-searching and a real belief that the Catholic Church is the true one.

Beside all these varying attitudes to religion, we see one which is total antagonism – that held by Cromwell, and imitated by Rich. Cromwell's priorities, as we know, are purely self-centred – 'convenience' for himself and the King, who rewards him. He sees personal morality – his own, Rich's, More's – as merely getting in the way, 'a shrill incessant pedagogue about its own salvation' (p. 93). He advises Rich to 'get sure' that he's not religious, for religion too gets in the way. And so Cromwell sets aside all scruples, twisting the law, the basic rules of society, his own conscience and Rich's to get what he wants. Therefore Cromwell is more than happy for Henry, if he wishes, to split from Rome, found his own Church, create his own Archbishop. Cromwell does anything to placate the King.

This brings us to the King himself, the instigator of the break with the Catholic Church. He certainly has a very sharp sense of morality, of what is right and wrong. We see in the Henry who talks to More in Act One a man who is almost painfully frightened of being immoral – so much so that he needs More's approval to act, and pushes More to his death when this approval is not forthcoming. Conversely, Henry's actions do seem motivated by a bewildering mixture of desires (some good and some bad): desire to have an heir, desire to ensure his country's stability, desire to see an uncorrupted Church, desire for Anne Boleyn. In the end, Henry, who so violently defended the Catholic Church in the past, breaks with Rome, and feels guilty about it; we suspect that his feelings are identical to More's, and that this is why he needs More's approval.

Thomas More himself, the central character of the play, is by definition our model for both personal morality and attitudes to religion. His personal morality is, as we have seen, steadfast; he is a gentle, kind man who uses his talents to the full for the glory of God, and relates to everyone with sensitivity. He nevertheless has the strength of character to follow his conscience, when everyone tries to persuade him otherwise, and chooses martyrdom rather than compromise.

It may be difficult, however, for us to see More's attitude to religion clearly; our present-day views are so very different from his. We may be able to understand why a man will die rather than betray his beliefs; but when those beliefs concern a deity who may not exist, represented on earth by a 'strikingly corrupt old person' (p. 44), then Thomas's stand seems a little less comprehensible.

The important thing to remember here is that Thomas is sure. He is sure God exists. He is sure that there is a direct route of spiritual guidance from God, through an unbroken line of Popes to the present one. He is sure, therefore, that if the Pope, however corrupt he may be, says that Henry cannot divorce Catherine, then this is so. It follows that Henry's divorcing Catherine is wrong – and it also follows that to break away from the Catholic Church is to cut the umbilical cord that links man with God's guidance. In the final analysis, therefore, when called on to agree with the divorce, Thomas cannot do so. And as he believes that God exists, he cannot swear otherwise without cutting himself off from God for all time – a prospect of unimaginable horror.

More's links with the Church are not those of an ignorant and uncritical person. More is an intelligent man who has thought through the issues. He knows and criticizes the Church's corruption and excesses. He sees clearly the false adulation of Chapuys for the outward signs: ''Tisn't "holy", Your Excellency; just old' (p. 50). At times, too, even his steady trust in God is shaken: 'I don't know where he is nor what he wants' (p. 39).

But ultimately, More simply and straightforwardly believes that God exists and shows himself in his Church. Everything else follows from this: the conversation with Henry, the silence, the refusal to take the oath, imprisonment and death – a death which shows us more clearly than anything else in the play that where morality and religion integrate in an individual conscience, the result is a whole, and holy, man.

Glossary

Adage: proverb
Ardent: zealous
Ascetic: austere
Avarice: greed
Barbarity: cruelty, savagery
Betoken: indicate, suggest
Bilked: cheated
Blithe: happy
Bounden: tied, fastened
Bracken: fern
Canon: ecclesiastical, Church
Chagrin: anger
Commodious: roomy
Common law: unwritten law derived from old law
Compulsion: obligation
Construe: interpret, expound, translate
Corroborate: confirm by evidence
Covert: hidden
Crave: beg
Debonair: pleasant
Degradation: debasement
Delineate: show
Demur: object
Deposition: sworn evidence
Dispatch: communication
Doff: take off
Enmity: hatred
Erupt: burst in

Excommunicate: someone expelled from the Church
Fastidious: particular
Fathom: measure
Forfeit: give up
Fortitude: courage
Glacial: icy
Gleeful: delighted
Gross: huge
Heinously: atrociously
Impeccably: faultlessly
Importunate: persistent
Incessant: increasing
Incognito: concealed
Infrangibly: unbreakably
Iniquitous: wicked, unjust
Instigate: urge on, incite
Irksome: tiresome
Jeer: mock
Jocosity: playfulness
Judicature: administration of justice
Judicially: legally
Licentious: lascivious
Liege: sovereign
Litigant: a contestant in law
Malevolent: wishing evil
Malignant: harmful
Maxim: principle
Megalomania: love of power
Mitigate: reduce

Murmuration: grumbling
Mutable: changeable
Nether: lower
Pedagogue: teacher
Perjure: swear falsely
Perturbed: agitated
Perverse: awkward
Pettish: petulant
Portentous: significant
Preamble: introduction
Pretension: assertion of a claim
Process: walk in procession
Pulmonary: of the lung
Punctiliously: formally, with attention
    to detail
Ratchet: toothed wheel
Rectitude: righteousness
Religiosity: religiousness
Rhetorical: impressive
Rigging: ship's masts and sails, trick-
    ing
Rigorous: severe
Ruminative: pondering

Sanction: penalty
Scrutinise: examine carefully
Sinew: muscle
Skiff: light rowing boat
Sloth: laziness
Solace: comfort
Spleen: ill-temper
Splenetic: ill-tempered
Statute: written law
Stricken: laid low
Suave: soothing
Superlatively: of the highest degree
Tangible: touchable
Temperate: moderate
Tenuous: subtle, weak
Truculent: aggressive
Unremitting: unceasing
Vestige: trace
Waspish: irritable
Whimsy: caprice
Windlass: machine for hoisting
Wrangling: arguing

Discussion Topics and Examination Questions

Discussion Topics

Your understanding and appreciation of the play will be much increased if you discuss aspects of it with other people. Here are some of the topics you can consider:

1. In what ways do you think that the title of the play does justice to the character of Sir Thomas More?

2. Despite the nature of the subject, say what you find humorous in the play and why.

3. Examine the characters of Alice and Margaret. What do their actions and reactions tell us about the character of More himself?

4. Consider the roles of Cromwell and Rich. Which of these two is the greater villain and why?

5. What opinions have you formed of Henry? Find evidence in the play to support your views.

6. What does the presentation of the Common Man contribute to the play?

7. What do you find the most exciting scene in the play and why?

8. Do you find the play pessimistic or optimistic? Examine it carefully and provide evidence from it to support your views.

9. What is the main theme of the play? When you have considered this, work out if there are other themes related to it or contrasting with it. (You might consider power, corruption, deception etc.)

10. Examine the importance of religion in the play.

11. 'Overall, a sad comment on human nature.' How far would you agree with this as an assessment of the play?

12. In what ways does Bolt succeed in giving us the realistic atmosphere of the period in *A Man for All Seasons*?

The GCSE Examination

If you are studying for the GCSE examination you may find that the set texts have been selected by your teacher from a very wide range of suggestions in the examination syllabus. The questions in the examination paper will therefore be applicable to many different books. Here are some possible questions which you could answer by making use of *A Man for All Seasons*:

1. In the book you are studying, show how any *two* characters change over the course of the story.

2. In your chosen book, write about the character of a man or woman whose life is based on truthfulness and principle.

3. Compare and contrast any two characters in your chosen book.

4. Write about the historical period in which a book you are studying is set, saying what effect it has on the lives of the main characters.

5. Write about the presentation of power or corruption in any book you have studied.

6. For which character in the book you are studying do you feel most sympathy and why?

7. In your chosen book, describe in detail any scene which has a sad or tragic impact.

8. Examine any relationship in the book you are reading. Show how it develops and indicate whether you consider it realistic or not.

9. In your chosen book, examine any character whose life is influenced by either (a) the nature of his/her work or (b) family responsibilities.

10. Write about any unusual aspect of the book you are studying.

11. In your chosen book, write an account of any scenes or situations which are humorous, saying why you find them so.

12. Write about a plan or a plot in the book you are reading, and say whether it is successful or not.